Ukraine Travel Guide.

Information Tourism

Author
Jesse Russell

First Printed: 2019.

Publisher:
SONITTEC LTD
College House, 2nd
Floor
17 King Edwards
Road,
Ruislip
London
HA4 7AE .

Table of Content

Summary

How Traveling Can Broaden Your Perspective

Ukraine Tourism: You may not need a lot of convincing when it comes to finding a reason to travel especially when considering a trip to a foreign country. Exploring the world, seeing new places, and learning about new cultures are just a few of the benefits of traveling. There is value to exploring someplace new and combating the stress of getting out of your comfort zone.

Traveling should be looked at as a journey for personal growth, mental health, and spiritual enlightenment. Taking the time to travel to a new place can both literally and figuratively open your eyes to things you have never seen before. These new experiences allow you to get to know yourself in ways you can't if you stay in the same place.

- ✓ Traveling is wonderful in so many ways:
- ✓ You can indulge your sense of wanderlust.
- ✓ You experience different cultures.
- ✓ Your taste buds get to experience unique foods.

✓ You meet all different kinds of people.

As you grow older, your mind evolves and expands to adapt to the new information you receive. Traveling to a new destination is similar in this way, but the learning process occurs at a faster rate. Traveling thrusts you into the unknown and delivers you with a bounty of new information and ideas. The expansion of your mind is one of the greatest benefits of travel. Keep reading to learn six more benefits of traveling.

> Discover Your Purpose: Feeling as though you have a purpose in life is more important than many people realize. A purpose connects you to something bigger than yourself and keeps you moving forward. Your purpose in life can change suddenly and fluidly as you enter new stages in becoming who you are. With each new stage in life, there comes new goals and callings. Traveling can help open your eyes to a new life direction. You may be wandering down a path unaware of where you will end up. Seeing new places and meeting new people can help you break from that path and discover what your true purpose is.

Traveling is an excellent remedy for when you feel you need to refocus on your purpose and goals, or re-evaluate your life path. There is no better time to open your eyes than when your life seems to be out of focus and in need of redirection. You might just be surprised by what you discover and find a new sense of life purpose how traveling changes you.

Traveling is a way to discover parts of yourself that you never knew existed. While traveling, you have no choice but to deal with unexpected situations. For example, how you may typically handle a problem at home might be a completely unacceptable approach when you are in an unfamiliar place without all of the comforts and conveniences of home.

> Be Aware of Your Blessings: When you travel to a new destination, your eyes are opened to new standards, and, you become more aware of all the blessings and privileges you have been given. It is easy to forget what you do have and only focus on what is missing from your life. Traveling can help put things back into perspective and re-center your priorities on what truly matters.

Consider traveling through an area that has no electricity or running water if you come from a place where cold bottled water is easily accessible and nearly anything you want can be delivered to your door in less than an hour. These are two completely different worlds and ways of living. For people who experience a more privileged quality of life, seeing others who live in drastically different situations can help you appreciate what you have and spark an interest for you to lend support to people living elsewhere.

> Find Truth: There's concept, and then there's experience. You can know things from reading them online and listening to a lecture, but to experience something in person is different.

Traveling can help open your eyes to the true kindness and goodness of humanity. There is a myth that when you travel you are on your own, but that simply is not the case. The welcoming attitude and overwhelming hospitality that people give to travelers may be one of the most surprising truths about traveling. Beyond that, you have the whole world to learn about with every place you discover, through every person you meet and every culture you experience.

> Expand Your Mind: A key benefit of traveling, or taking the opportunity to explore on a vacation, is being given the opportunity to expand your mind in ways you can't imagine. If you can allow yourself to travel with an open mind and accept the new experiences and adventures around you, you give your mind the chance to see the world from a new perspective.

Think of it as a spiritual and intellectual enlightenment. You never stop being curious and should always seek out education whenever possible throughout your life. You are doing a disservice to yourself if you choose to close yourself off from the world. It is not always easy to let new ideas in, especially when they are in direct contrast with what you may believe. You have everything you need to grow, you just have to allow yourself to do it.

> Connect to Others: It's easy to forget how similar you are to others, regardless of where you come from, what your background is, or how much money you have. At the end of the day, human beings share more in common with one another than they may choose to admit. When taking a trip to a different country, you may have learned to cast aside what is different and unusual because from the outside, others may not look or act alike. But if you give yourself a chance, you may be surprised to find how minimal and superficial these differences are.

As you notice how you share similar needs, your perspective of your home expands, you become friends with people from different backgrounds and cultures, you realize how everyone is connected. This state of awareness is a jump in consciousness that can help you experience a world-centric view of consciousness more expansive and aware.

> Break Out of Your Shell: Without a doubt, one of the benefits of traveling is that it forces you to step out of your bubble, which can provide you with many emotional health benefits. Yes, it may be uncomfortable and scary to break away from your daily routine, but the rewards are worth it. What you gain in experience and knowledge may outweigh any amount of doubt or apprehension you had before embarking on your journey. Travel also helps you to self-reflect and dig deep into who you are as a person.

Something magical happens when people are put in new situations than they are normally faced with in their everyday life, as behavior becomes more raw and real as a result of being out of your conditioned environment. This not-so-subtle push into the world helps you to become more open and comfortable expressing yourself without the worry of feeling judged.

> See the Big Picture: Life is a limited gift. You must choose to make the most of each day. As you travel and experience more of the world, you may be struck with gratitude and appreciation for all the places you have enjoyed and people you've shared your travels with. You have the power to take control of your life and can inspire you to start doing more.

About Ukraine
Ukraine Introduction

Vast and mysterious to many, Ukraine is barely known to outsiders despite being one of the largest countries in Europe. Long-associated with its colossal neighbour Russia, it's a country that stands out in its own right for its varied landscapes and surprising cultural diversity.

To the majority of those visiting for the first time, the reputation of Ukraine's hardy inhabitants can seem formidable. But while, much like in neighbouring Russia, cracking a smile at a stranger in the street is deemed a sure sign of madness, locals tend to be a thoroughly welcoming lot once you've broken the ice. Before long they'll be showing you round the sights and inviting you to their home for a steaming borscht the country's iconic beetroot soup.

Ukraine's natural side is also seen as tough and it's true that in winter snow covers most of the land as temperatures plummet. During the rest of the year, though, it's surprisingly clement. What's more, with its largely unspoilt, verdant interior, Ukraine is ideal for hikers and cyclists.

The Carpathian Mountains that spill over the border with Poland, Hungary and Romania dominate the west of the country while flat plains carpeted with sunflowers and cereals make up much of the central and eastern region. To the south are the almost Mediterranean-like Black Sea coast and the Crimean Peninsula, which remains a huge draw for holidaymakers every summer. And even when snow falls through the winter, the landscape is beautiful, while there are many old churches and Soviet-era buildings to dive into for shelter.

Ukraine's capital, Kiev, founded in the eighth century, displays a heady mix of architecture befitting of a city that was once capital of Kievan Rus, the precursor of the modern Russian state. A wealth of baroque and Renaissance architecture can also be found in Lviv, one of Europe's oldest cities, while Odessa is probably best known for the Potemkin Stairway that featured in Sergei Eisenstein's epic film The Battleship Potemkin.

Recently, Ukraine has been in the news for the wrong reasons due to Russian separatism on the border. Despite this, most of the country is completely safe for visitors.

Country guide

Sightseeing

Ukraine sightseeing. Travel guide attractions, sights, nature and touristic places

A country of rich history, Ukraine carefully keeps and preserves its cultural heritage, and never ceases to attract travelers with its diversity and numerous fascinating landmarks. Nearly every city of Ukraine is interesting and original. Naturally, the majority of places of interest are located in Kiev. The Golden Gate is considered the symbol of the city. Many centuries ago this was the main entrance to Kiev. The gate is decorated with copper and gilding, so the arc looks truly elegant. In the 18th century new buildings were constructed around the gate. The gate lost its original meaning and was, consequently, destroyed. Nowadays the landmark was reconstructed, and the ruins of the original gate can be seen behind the new one.

Kiev Pechersk Lavra is one more irreplaceable symbol of Kiev. This is a large complex of religious buildings, the history of which starts in 1051. This is the year when monks started transforming caves into monasteries and temples. It took as long as nine centuries to turn an empty space on the right bank of the Dnepr River into a beautiful complex of magnificent churches and monasteries. Kiev Pechersk Lavra suffered great damage during the years of World War II, for example, the reconstruction of the Uspensky Cathedral was finished only in 2000. Nowadays, this magnificent complex has not only religious but also great cultural importance as many of its buildings are true architectural landmarks.

Ukraine is famous for its beautiful parks and nature reserves. Yevpatoria is one of the most beautiful and picturesque cities in the country. It is famous for its wonderful pedestrian zones, parks and walkways. The only dinopark in the country was also opened in Yevpatoria not long ago. As one can guess from the name, the main exhibition of dinopark is dedicated to dinosaurs. During an excursion there, visitors will learn many interesting facts about first inhabitants of the planet and see many precious archaeological findings. There are also several attractions, restaurants and playgrounds on the territory of the complex.

Stryjski Park, which is located in Lviv, is one of the most famous nature landmarks in the country. The park was founded in 1877 and occupies the area of approximately 60 hectares. It is included in the top 10 list of the most beautiful parks in Europe. In Stryjski Park visitors will see numerous rare trees and bushes, blooming flower beds and cozy summer houses. There is a wonderful lake not far away from the entrance, where one can see beautiful swans during warmer months of the year. The design of the park is changed throughout the year, so it looks new every time you visit it.

History and Entertainment

Besides multiple excursions, the guests of Ukraine can take part in many other interesting entertainments. The Ukrainian Carpathians are a place where popular ski resorts are located. The most famous of them are Dragobrat, Bukovel and Yaremche. Despite the fact that the weather here is mild in winter, the resort season lasts for about 5 months. At the resorts, there are ski routes of different levels. Absolutely all resorts are suitable for families with children. Special playgrounds are equipped for younger guests. At the resorts, there are also slopes for sledding and places for other winter entertainments.

In summer period, the resorts located in the mountains are very interesting too. There are perfect conditions for active holidays. Tourists have an opportunity to take part in hiking and bike rides. There are also excellent riding centers at the resorts. Ukraine is famous for its wellness resorts. Some treatment centers and pensions have been working for many years.

The country is notable for its healing mineral springs and firth lakes where healing mud and brine are produced. Here, adherents of the health tourism are offered to try unique therapeutic methods based on the use of natural components. For the health tourism, you can choose Berdyansk or Polyana. Excellent historical treatment centers are located in Odessa and Truskavets.

The pride of Ukraine is national food traditions. The Ukrainian cuisine is very practical and nourishing. Some of the most popular national dishes are Ukrainian beet-root soup and pork fat that has long become an important food symbol of the country. Pork fat is cooked in many ways. The classic dish is salty, smoked and marinated fat.

Dumplings are also a popular national dish. They are served with dozens of different fillings. Gourmets should certainly walk along food stores in big cities where you can buy amazing fillings prepared by historical recipes. They are cooked of fruit and berries. Fillings with different medicinal herbs are very popular with tourists. Another national beverage is mead that is also one of the most popular souvenirs.

Cities and regions

Alupka
Guide to Alupka
Sightseeing in Alupka what to see. Complete travel guide
The real highlight and characteristic feature of Alupka is the rich vegetation, tangled and winding city streets, the beauty of the Vorontsov Palace and the amazing park. And yet, of course, the majestic peaks of Ai-Petri mountain, which are impossible to forget after seeing them at least once.

The history of Alupka began in 960, when the Crimea was under the rule of the Khazar Khaganate. A settlement called Alubika was founded here. These places have preserved the memory of different historical eras up to our time. On the South Coast of Crimea, scientists have discovered the ruins of Taurian burial grounds with tombs and fortresses. Over the years, the population of the southern coast has lost its relative independence. By order of the emperor of Byzantium Justinian I, "long walls" were erected on the mountain passes. The walls were supposed to stop nomads and block the access to these lands.

The former Taurian citadels were gradually strengthened, new fortresses called "Isara" were erected. The ruins of the watchtowers and Isara fortresses could be seen in the immediate vicinity of Alupka till the end of the 19th century. The very first settlement on the site of modern Alupka dates back to the VIII century BC.

In the XIV-XV centuries, a one of the strongholds of the Genoese was located here, it was called Lupiko. After the annexation of Crimea to the Russian Empire in 1783, Alupka was given in possession to Prince Potemkin. Later, in 1823, it was taken over by Count Vorontsov, who built the legendary palace here. Nowadays, Vorontsov Palace is the main attraction of the city.

In the XX century, Alupka becomes a popular resort, at this time more than 200 private resorts are being built on its territory. It is worth noting that Maxim Gorky, Fyodor Chaliapin, Ivan Bunin, Mikhail Kotsyubinsky, Sergey Rachmaninov, Lesya Ukrainka and other famous celebrities have vacationed in Alupka. In 1938, Alupka acquired the status of a city, and in 1941, it already had 25 health resorts of various profiles, several schools, a hospital, and other institutions.

Alupka is beautiful at any time of the year, including the winter period. At any time, visitors are always welcome here. The doors of guest houses, hotels and recreation centers are open to visitors all year round. It is worth noting that the majority of tourists in the winter come here to improve their health by the re-healing air, which has a proven effect on health conditions. In winter, there are few holidaymakers in the resort, and therefore a very calm and relaxing atmosphere reigns.

The important religious monument at the resort is the Church of Archangel Michael that started to be built in 1898. It was constructed on the ruins of the old church, which preserved some elements used for the foundation afterwards. The new church was finally built in 1903 and reconstructed not so long ago. Today, the temple attracts with its big golden domes. The church facade has remained almost unchangeable since its construction.

At the resort, there are also a lot of unique nature attractions. One of its districts bears a quite unusual name - Big and Small Chaos. This is an area where natural stone formations were found. The researchers still argue about how this area appeared. This interesting district is not so far from the Vorontsov Palace. As some researchers suppose, it was formed by the volcanic eruption.

The special cultural center in the city is the Theatre of Sea Animals. The diversity of animal species, whose performances you can witness in the theatre, is really impressive. Every day, a lot of interesting events are held here. The theatre is located on the territory of the beautiful park. In it, there is also another unusual attraction, the inverted house. Everyone can visit it too. It is necessary to be very careful inside the house, as all the items of furniture are turned upside down here.

Those who prefer walking along picturesque places should certainly take tours to the waterfall on the river Uchan-su. It is located in the incredibly beautiful natural area. When moving towards to the waterfall, you can admire fabulous landscapes and see rare plants and typical dwellers of this place. Experienced tourists note that it is more interesting to admire the waterfall in spring when it becomes very swift.

The main value of the historical resort is the Massandara winery that you can visit too. The visitors of the winery have an opportunity to watch how legendary wine is produced and to see the halls where wine is vatted. On its territory, there is a tasting room where you can taste the most popular wine. Here, you can also drop in a specialized shop.

Alushta

Guide to Alushta

Sightseeing in Alushta what to see. Complete travel guide

One of the most ancient and charming cities of the Southern Coast of Crimea, Alushta strikes with its extraordinary beauty, compact size and amazing nature. Once, there was a very ordinary small village. It was at the intersection of several important trade routes, and therefore developed very rapidly. Until now, scientists and archaeologists exploring this settlement of ancient Taurus cannot come to an unequivocal opinion regarding the emergence of roads from multi-ton stone slabs, which were not afraid of dirt, slush, or other weather phenomena.

In the 6th century AD, the area where Alushta is now located, like the entire Southern Coast of Crimea, was under the rule of the mighty Byzantine Empire - the great heiress of Ancient Rome. It was at that time that the stone fortress Aluston was built near the sea shore, which was supposed to protect the land from sea robbers. In modern Alushta you can see the ruins of the ancient tower of Ashagi-kul, an important historical site.

For a long time, Alushta was under the rule of the Byzantines, after - the Genoese, and also the Crimean Tatars, but the most intense and interesting part of its history begins after the annexation of Crimea to the Russian Empire. At that time, the population of Alushta was about 250 people who were engaged in manual labor - cattle breeding, farming and fishing. The construction of a road from Simferopol to Alushta had very strong impact on the development of the city. Already at the end of the XIX century Alushta became a popular resort village.

In the time of Tsarist Russia, many noblemen built mansions here. Wealthy people, representatives of nobility and bohemians preferred to come to rest in Alushta. The public resort of Alushta already was in the Soviet era; it was during this period that most sanatoriums, boarding houses and health resorts were built here. Here ordinary people could rest, and a unique trolleybus route was built from Simferopol to Alushta. Now, it is an attractive modern resort with developed infrastructure, lots of parks, entertainment, attractive sea and air. People who come here to rest come from all parts of the former Soviet Union. Alushta provides an opportunity to organize a vacation at any affordable price.

One of the most visited places in Alushta is the local Aquarium opened in 2003. Initially, it was quite small but, within just a few years, the collection of sea dwellers was so enlarged that it has become the largest on the coast of Crimea. Today, there are 4 spacious halls where you can see aquariums with exotic fish and other dwellers of the sea depths. Some of the representatives of the marine fauna are very rare.

At the resort, there is the interesting Park of Miniatures. It offers its visitors to look at the small copies of the famous attractions of the region. Crimea in Miniature includes copies of such famous attractions, as the Vorontsov Palace, the Swallow's Nest fortress, Funa, etc. This unusual outdoor museum was built on the territory of the beautiful park. All its extraordinary constructions are hidden by exotic plants.

The important religious attraction at the resort is the Church of All Crimean Saints built in the middle of the 19th century. The architecture of this temple is very different from other churches built in the same period. To construct it, a famous architect from Odessa was invited. He decided to implement his project in the style of English rural churches. If taking into account that the Gothic style came back into "architecture fashion" again, the exterior of the church gained quite unusual features.

In the vicinity of the resort, there is the amazing Crimean Natural Reserve. It is famous for its natural beauties and attractions. On its territory, there are several dozens of hiking routes stretching along the fabulous mountainous areas. In the reserve, there are a lot of rare trees, some of which are aged over a hundred years.

There are also many interesting historical attractions, including the Monastery of Kosma and Damian. It was founded in 1856. In the period of the Great Patriotic War, the monastery was destroyed almost completely. It started being restored only in 1994. Nowadays, you can take excursions around the entire territory of the monastery and learn about its fascinating history.

Culture: sights to visit

Culture of Alushta. Places to visit old town, temples, theaters, museums and palaces

Alushta is one of the oldest and most beautiful cities of Crimea, located in a picturesque corner of the island, which at one time was visited by many famous personalities. Guests of Alushta have a worthy choice of sights and interesting cultural sites for studying. One of the most visited places is the "Museum of Marine Disasters", which is not in Alushta itself, but not far from it - in the village of "Malorechenskoye". It is a unique memorial complex dedicated to the memory of those who died at sea.

The museum itself is located in the "St. Nicholas church of Myra", which is also one of the important sights. The tower of the church performs the function of a lighthouse - the highest on the territory of Crimea. The design of the museum is interesting, and everything here is devoted to the marine theme. There is also a remarkable exhibition area, made in the form of the famous Flying Dutchman with a real captain's bridge and graceful sails.

In the very center of Alushta is located the "Church of All Saints" - the most remarkable architectural monument, built in the Gothic style. Its construction was conducted under the leadership of Count Vorontsov.

Restoration of the temple was held in 1991, and now over its central entrance, towers a three-tiered bell tower, which looks very elegant in the background of "Mount Demiredzhi". "Alushta Museum of Local History" will be of interest to history lovers. The very building of the museum is also part of the history, since it was built in the beginning of the 19th century. The museum has many interesting archaeological finds, there are rare documents and photographs, but it is especially interesting to study objects of everyday life, their clothes and household items.

The oldest building on the territory of the modern resort is the "fortress of Aluston"; to this day only fragments of a large fortification structure have been preserved. There are ruins right in the center of the city and they produce a somewhat strange impression, as they are surrounded on all sides by modern buildings and household buildings. Outside the city, right next to the mountain peak of Shagan-Kaya is one of the most amazing city attractions - "Gazebo of winds". The arbor was built in 1956 and consists of several columns and a dome, whose height is about 4 meters; on the floor you can see the mosaic pattern of the Wind Rose.

Attractions & nightlife

City break in Alushta. Active leisure ideas for Alushta attractions, recreation and nightlife

In Alushta you can rest in different ways. Here you can sunbathe and have fun all day on one of the beaches, and in the evening, walk through the wonderful streets of the city, the waterfront or the center, enjoying the sounds of music, as well as the colorful lights of bars and restaurants. For lovers of outdoor activities and extreme entertainment in the resort too, were created excellent conditions. For those who prefer to spend much of their time on the beaches, Alushta is ideal. Large pebble beach predominates here. They are well-equipped and suitable for both active and serene leisure. Fans of diving can dive with scuba-diving off the wonderful coast of Alushta, which is famous for its diversity of marine life.

For those who wish to diversify the beach vacation with unusual entertainment, it is worth going to the tasting room at the "Tavrida" factory. This is a real find for connoisseurs of fine wines. Here for the visitors very informative excursions are conducted, and after that they invite you to a cozy hall where you can try the best drinks. Numerous entertainment centers invite people to play billiards, table tennis or slot machines. The most colorful and interesting is the entertainment complex "Halloween".

For lovers of extreme types of recreation, the best entertainment center will be the water park "Almond Grove". Here you can relax in comfort all day. The water park is a well-developed infrastructure. Already almost traditional for those who like to relax actively, there are trips on horses to the mountains, liked at the resort by lovers of hiking and cycling. Also, vacationers are given the opportunity to rent a jeep and ride on inaccessible mountain roads of Big Alushta.

In the evening, the liveliest place of the resort is the embankment, which will fit perfectly for romantic walks under the moon. Lovers of loud music and dancing can go to the nightclub "Pashera", which is considered the most popular of its kind in the resort. For travelers who are accustomed to spending evenings in a more relaxed atmosphere, a cinema with an unusual name "Storm" is more suitable for a rest. Its rich poster is designed for a wide range of visitors.

Cuisine & restaurants

Cuisine of Alushta for gourmets. Places for dinner best restaurants
Alushta is a popular resort town with a lot of bars and restaurants. There are cookery institutions of different directions and price level, so everyone can choose a suitable place for rest. For those who are unpretentious to food and want to save money, it is worth paying attention to self-service café - an analogue of the former Soviet canteens. All of them are located on the waterfront. One of the most popular places where food is really quality, and the prices are affordable, is the canteen "Po-domashnemu". It is located in the center of the embankment and is in demand not only among tourists, but also among locals.

If it is about dinner, which should be special and memorable, then it is worth paying attention to the popular cafes and restaurants of Alushta. A real local attraction is the restaurant "Pekin", built in the form of a Chinese pagoda. This is a popular Chinese restaurant with impeccable service and a stylish menu. The restaurant is aimed at wealthy visitors, who are many among the guests of the resort. Also, one of the most attractive restaurants in the city is the "Vstrecha"; it specializes in cooking Italian cuisine and is ideal for tasting fine Italian wine. Prices here are also above average, but for a huge number of visitors this does not affect.

Fans of a variety of culinary trends will find Alushta a suitable place for recreation. Lovers of Russian cuisine will be able to taste roast pig, sturgeon, traditional Russian okroshka and ordinary pelmeni cooked according to old recipes. Those who prefer Ukrainian cuisine should endeavor to try the delicious Ukrainian borsch with pampushkas, lard, vareniki with a variety of fillings and pancakes with cottage cheese. No less remarkable is the Tatar cuisine, which is very diverse here. In any Tatar cafe, guests will be offered excellent shish-kebab from lamb, soup from peas and beans "bakla shorba", noodles with vegetables under meat sauce and many other interesting dishes. It is impossible to imagine local restaurants without classic pilaf, manti and lagman.

Traditions & lifestyle
Colors of Alushta traditions, festivals, mentality and lifestyle

Alushta is one of the most modern cities of the Crimean peninsula, which managed to preserve the unique charm of the past. The city has a lot of interesting features, which must be noted by attentive travelers. Narrow streets, through which public transport hardly advances, do not go unnoticed. By the way, drive here is at a frenzied speed, even in very winding streets, and so a ride on a local taxi is a separate attraction. Those who go to Alushta by private car should be especially careful, local drivers "do not forgive" inexperienced tourists for their carelessness.

As for the character of the locals, they are quite sympathetic and hospitable. Before asking for help from the citizens, you should definitely say hello; during communication, do not forget about the elementary courtesy. Speaking about the culture of locals, it is worth mentioning the traditions of wine making, which totals more than one hundred years. Here, wine is treated very respectfully. Many locals themselves know how to cook it perfectly, and it turns out they are no worse than the factory ones. The tourists have a great value for home wine, but it should be chosen attentively and carefully.

You can fully experience the unique atmosphere of the national color during a walk through one of the city's markets. There is always a very lively atmosphere; voices are heard everywhere and mountains (literally) of fresh vegetables and fruits are visible. It is worth noting that the indigenous people prefer to go shopping in markets, although the choice of supermarkets in the resort is also very large. For many townspeople, going to the market has become a good tradition. The attitude towards the sea among the indigenous people, on the contrary, is rather restrained. Not all regularly rest on the beach; this way of organizing leisure for locals is more an exception than a usual event. The atmosphere of the city is constantly changing, but it manages to maintain its national attractiveness and unique charm.

Tips for tourists

Preparing your trip to Alushta: advices & hints things to do and to obey

1. An alternative to local inns and hotels can be houses and apartments, which the locals willingly rent out to visitors. If you prefer a private apartment, do not agree to the first offer, the choice of housing in Alushta is very large, as well as the range of prices. The peak prices here are in August and early September. The price of accommodation depends on living conditions, as well as proximity to the sea.

2. Buy Crimean wine on the streets with hands with great care. Experienced travelers recommend going to choose a wine in one of the local specialized stores, such shops have all brands of wines.

3. Resting on the beach, never leave your things unattended as one of the main problems of the resort are thieves. Do not take large sums of money or valuables with you without the need.

4. Do not buy food on the beaches with hands, it is also very risky. It is best to take suitable food with you or go to one of the local cafes. All fruits and vegetables bought in the market or in the store must be washed thoroughly.

5. A real find for holidaymakers will be small street tents and cafes, in which chebureks and a lot of other popular treats are sold. Chebureks in Alushta are prepared the largest in the Crimea, and the prices for them always remain attractive.

6. In Alushta, there is only one free beach - Central, and for entering the territory of other beaches you need to pay a small amount. As a rule, it already includes a fee for the use of sun loungers and beach umbrellas, so the size of payment is fully justified.

7. Alushta is in demand by travelers not only in summer but also in winter. It is worth going there for those who wish to celebrate the New Year in an unusual atmosphere. It is worth noting that in winter the choice of entertainment for the guests of the resort is also very large.

8. On the territory of the resort, it is convenient to move on foot and the main types of public transport in Alushta are shuttle buses. The fare directly depends on the distance, so it is best to specify it in advance.

9. Another popular mode of transport is trolleybuses. On trolleybus number 51 vacationers can get to Simferopol. Also, it is worth considering that the trolleybus is the cheapest type of transport, a trip by shuttle bus or bus will cost about one and a half to two times more.

Chernivtsi

Guide to Chernivtsi

Sightseeing in Chernivtsi what to see. Complete travel guide
Chernivtsi is a big cultural center of Western Ukraine that is inferior only to Lviv in the number of excursion objects. The formation of the cultural traditions of the city was influenced by different countries. Throughout its history, it has been a part of different countries. The first references to Chernivtsi date back to the beginning of the 15th century. Moldavia, Poland, the Ottoman Empire, Romania and Austria-Hungary alternately struggled for the city.

Every country contributed much to the development of the prospective city. For example, Chernivtsi has its incomparable appearance thanks to Austrian masters. In the period between the 17th-18th centuries, they built a lot of wonderful architectural complexes in Chernivtsi. Some of the buildings have been preserved to this day in their original form. Due to the plenty of unique architectural monuments, Chernivtsi was unofficially called "Small Paris". It is a really beautiful and enchanting city with its unique and interesting culture.

It has long attracted many travelers. The resort is attractive for tourists from Europe because of its close proximity to Romania. It is popular with fans of excursions and hiking. The guests come here for interesting attractions and favorable weather conditions that are perfect for active holidays. Chernivtsi has another attractive feature, affordable prices. You can rent an excellent room at the middle-level hotel for a moderate price. If you pay a little more, you can stay at the most luxurious hotel with all the amenities.

The city is perfect for travelers with children. There are many beautiful places for family recreation, affordable restaurants and very interesting entertainment centers. The picturesque resort will also impress adherents of the food tourism. In the city, there are many restaurants of the Austrian, Romanian, Ukrainian, and Russian cuisine. Those who choose a national restaurant should certainly taste gutsulski banosh, a popular meat dish of the best pork, cottage cheese and sour cream. Chernivtsi has everything to surprise its guests. Your vacation in this enchanting and romantic city will never be boring.

The city is a real trove of historical attractions. In Chernivtsi, there is the preserved Khotyn Fortress. It was built in the 13th century to protect the territory. In the 16th century, the fortress was rebuilt completely and broadened. In 1621, the fortress went through the unique battle against the Turkish troop of over 250 000 people. The fight lasted for over a month but Turkish conquerors did not manage to conquer the fortress. Actually, the impregnable construction protected Europe from the future invasions of the Ottoman Empire. The historical monument has been preserved to this day perfectly. Films are often made on its territory.

The beautiful religious monument is Church of St. Paraskevi. It was built in the 15th century. Originally, the church was built of wood. In the 19th century, it was rebuilt of stone. The temple the city guests can see today was finished in 1860. It resembles classic Serbian temples. Today, one of the main peculiarities of the church is its beautiful black domes.

Another interesting historical site is the Organ Hall located in the building of the old Armenian church. This beautiful building was built of red brick in the second half of the 19th century. It is an impressive combination of Byzantium and Gothic styles. After the Revolution in 1917 and the enthronement of the Soviet authority, the church was closed and came to the philharmonic. Now, the historic building serves as a concert hall, as it is distinguished by incredible acoustics. Organ music concerts of famous musicians from different countries are regularly held here.

In the city, there is the wonderful Botanical Garden that will impress all nature admirers. It was set up in 1877 and belongs to the Chernivtsi State University. During the Great Patriotic War, the garden was almost destroyed. Right after the War, it started to be renovated. In

1963, the garden was recognized as an attraction of national significance. Today, you can see here the rich collection of tropical plants. There is also a modern library where selection experiments are conducted. In a warm period, you can see a lot of beautiful landscape attractions and flower beds in the garden.

Dnepropetrovsk

Guide to Dnepropetrovsk

Sightseeing in Dnepropetrovsk what to see. Complete travel guide
Dnipropetrovsk is one of the most beautiful cities in Ukraine. The locals call it simply Dnieper, since the city is located in the central part of the country, just on the bank of the river with the same name. It is an industrial city with a rich history. The earliest fortification settlements were founded on this territory in the 16th century, which was due to the insecurity of the southern borders of the Polish-Lithuanian Commonwealth. As known, then the Taurian steppes freely moved the Tatar hordes, attacking small settlements and ruining cities.

The first real city in this territory was founded much later, in 1776, by the decree of Catherine the Great. It was founded by Prince Grigory Potemkin, one of the favorites of the Empress, so it was quite natural that he called the city Yekaterinoslav. This is how the city was called until 1926. At the beginning of the 20th century, it acquired the status of a major industrial center. The city's territory had advanced metallurgical and machine-building factories, and in the middle of the 20th century the first rocket-building factory was opened here.

For many years the advanced industrial center remained closed, and it was necessary to obtain a special permit to enter its territory as well as for leaving the city. The city became accessible to travelers only recently. In Dnipropetrovsk there are historical, artistic and literary museums, as well as numerous centers of modern culture. In a large city there are about 2200 streets and 94 thousand different buildings. There are also unique historical sites, which are more than 200 years old.

The main entertainment for tourists remains visiting historical sites and sightseeing, which in the city is a great variety. One of the first architectural complexes that deserve attention is the Transfiguration Cathedral, erected in the beginning of the 19th century by the order of Catherine II. The church was built by the best architects; it is of great value not only as a historical object, but also as an artifact. The best example of classicism was recognized by the St. Nicholas Church, the halls of which are adorned with beautiful murals. Among the religious buildings there is also the Bryansk Nikolaev church, built in 1915.

The Potemkin Palace, located in the center of one of the parks deserves attention. The best architects and architects, led by I. Starova, worked on the palace project. Today its main part has been transformed into a palace of culture, exhibitions and expositions of young artists, poetry evenings and theatrical performances take place here.

The highest building in Dnipropetrovsk and a real masterpiece of modern architecture is the residential complex "Tower", whose height is 123 meters. There is the longest building in the city, located on the Heroes Avenue. The length of the building is 830 meters, which corresponds to the distance between two trolleybus stops.

The most interesting place in the city is the Monastery Island. According to historical data, many outstanding personalities have visited here, including Andrey Pervozvanny, Princess Olga and Prince Vladimir the Great.

Near the park you can see the building of the Hotel "Ukraine", which was built in 1912. Initially, a theater was located here, but after the revolution of 1917, the building was converted into a hotel complex. Today, only part of the distant wing is converted into a theater room.

You can get acquainted with the history of Dnipropetrovsk during an excursion to the Historical Museum and the Museum of Antiquity. You can relax from numerous excursions in one of the picturesque parks, most of which were broken up in the last century. There are also several monuments and memorials dedicated to great artists and politicians on their territory.

Nature admirers will be certainly impressed by the Botanical Garden of Dnipropetrovsk National University. Now, you can see several thousand plant species on its territory. Most of them are really exotic and untypical for this area. In a warm season, many plants start to bloom in the garden. The founder of the garden is professor Reinhard. He planted the first trees here in 1931.

For the first 30 years of its existence, the collection of the garden has been expanded significantly. In 1963, it was declared a natural reserve. Several years ago, the special exhibition center was opened in the garden. Here, you can buy beautiful decorative plants and flowers. It is better to check the time when you can visit the garden in advance, as it is not opened 7 days a week.

Culture: sights to visit

Culture of Dnepropetrovsk. Places to visit old town, temples, theaters, museums and palaces

Dnipropetrovsk will please fans of fascinating excursions with a rich choice of historical and architectural monuments. The city has many interesting museums, galleries and theaters. One of the most beautiful architectural structures is the "Transfiguration Cathedral", the construction of which began in 1830 and lasted almost five years. The church was completely restored in 1975 and today it is one of the most significant historical sites of the country.

No less interesting excursion facility is the "church of St. Nicholas", erected in the early 19th century. In the middle of the 17th century the first wooden church appeared on its place, and a hundred years later it was decided to destroy it and erect a stone building in the classical style. A beautiful stone building in the style of classicism has survived to this day in its pristine condition. Immediately after the completion of construction, its walls were adorned with skilful paintings, which visitors can still admire today. According to historical data, the first religious building on the site of the modern cathedral appeared in the middle of the 17th century. Over time, the wooden church decayed and in its place it was decided to erect a larger construction of stone.

On the territory of a beautiful park is the "Potemkin Palace"- a magnificent architectural monument of the late 18th century. At present, the beautiful building is a palace of culture; its main building includes several beautiful ceremonial rooms and halls, which are excellent for holding ceremonial events. After viewing the beautiful palace, vacationers will be offered a walk in the park, which has long become a favorite vacation spot for townspeople and visitors.

To later monuments of architecture should be attributed hotel "Ukraine". The building, which now houses the hotel complex, was built in 1912. Until 1917 it housed the theater "Palace", and later it was decided to open the hotel. Part of the historical building is still used today for theater performances.

The most interesting cultural institution of Dnipropetrovsk is the Historical Museum. It was founded in 1849 and was called the Museum of Antiquities. An invaluable collection of historical artifacts was repeatedly transported from one building to another and since 1903 it has been located in a beautiful palace. Recently a new building was added to the historic building, which housed a collection of artifacts dedicated to the battle for Dnieper - one of the most important historical events in the life of the city. Connoisseurs of theatrical art should definitely visit the "theater of Shevchenko", which regularly hosts bright premieres and beloved theatrical productions.

Attractions & nightlife

*City break in Dnepropetrovsk. Active leisure ideas for
Dnepropetrovsk attractions, recreation and nightlife*
Dnipropetrovsk boasts of a rich choice of not only cultural attractions, but also various entertainment facilities. Numerous clubs await music lovers and dancers, each of which prepares for visitors an interesting evening program. In the Augustin club visitors can not only enjoy their favorite music and dance, but also play billiards, as well as visit an attractive restaurant. The club bar offers a huge selection of exotic drinks. Only author's cocktails here are more than one hundred.

Fans of colorful parties and popular music will like the Labyrinth Club, which is located near the city center. Several times a week there are interesting parties and performances of popular disc jockeys. Those who want to relax in a secluded atmosphere and enjoy special treats are provided with a cozy lounge.

Entertainment complex "Vodogray" is very popular among tourists. It has an excellent swimming pool and sauna, a banquet room for celebrations and karaoke, as well as a cozy billiard room and a bar.

Sports fans will not lack choice of places for recreation. Traditional sports centers and all kinds of playgrounds are also available for guests of the city, and lovers of fishing can go to the most "fish places". On the waterfront, you can book a night fishing trip or rent a yacht and go on a romantic cruise. In summer, several attractive beaches are open on the banks of the Dnieper; lovers of sunbathing will not be disappointed either.

Fans of outdoor recreation like walking in the park Shevchenko. On its territory there are also several entertainment facilities, among which the Aquarium. It is home to a wide variety of freshwater fish and turtles, as well as more exotic inhabitants of the underwater world. There are more than twenty high-quality cinemas in the city. In each of which there are often the most popular and bright modern films. Many picturesque streets and parks are at the disposal of fans of hiking. One of the most attractive is the park named after Lazarus Globa.

Colorful shopping complexes, as well as numerous souvenir shops and antique shops awaits lovers of shopping. It is worth visiting the Central Department Store, which presents a huge selection of the most diverse stores. A significant part of popular shopping complexes is located near the city center. For memorable souvenirs you can go to the embankment or visit the Garnet store, which offers not only interesting crafts, but also antiques for sale.

Cuisine & restaurants

Cuisine of Dnepropetrovsk for gourmets. Places for dinner best restaurants

Rest in Dnipropetrovsk will be incomplete without visiting local restaurants; the city offers many cafes and restaurants for every taste. Some features of local cuisine here are hard to figure out, because they eat everything, based on their financial capabilities and priorities.

One of the most unusual establishments in the city is the restaurant complex "Reporter", in incomparable interior of which several epochs were embodied at once. The location of the restaurant complex is a stylish three-storey building of triangular shape. On the first floor, there is a bar where you can drink a mug of cold beer and watch a sports match. On the second floor, there is an attractive coffee house, where you can find refined coffee and wonderful sweets. At the highest floor there is a stylish restaurant where you can order dishes of Russian and Ukrainian cuisine prepared according to the author's recipes.

Another very unusual establishment in Dnipropetrovsk is the restaurant "Sakura". Classical Japanese cuisine with a delicious assortment of sushi and rolls is presented here, and the prices are very low and will please any visitor. In addition to a rich menu, the restaurant is ready to offer its customers a lot of interesting entertainment. It features a beautiful dance floor and a karaoke room.

Gourmets, who prefer French cuisine, will definitely like the restaurant "Saint-Tropez", there is always a harmonious and pacifying atmosphere in its charming hall. The high-class restaurant has an excellent choice of drinks; the basis of the wine list is made up of the most popular French wines. Here you can try the foie gras, cooked in the best traditions of French cuisine, hot buns melting in the mouth, as well as branded almond parfait. Among the cafes in the city, "Amphora" deserves special attention. This cozy place is perfect for people of all ages and culinary preferences. For solemn events there is a beautiful hall and small guest's cafe which offers a special menu with an abundance of interesting treats. There is an excellent bar in the stylish cafe and, also visitors can purchase meals to takeaway. In the city there are several hundred gastronomic institutions, and each of them is unique in its own way.

On the embankment of Lenin is the August restaurant, which is very popular among travelers. The establishment specializes in the preparation of national dishes. Several times a week, interesting events are organized for guests. On Mondays, there are discounts on desserts, and on Thursdays visitors can order the best fish dishes at a 20% discount. Fans of seafood will like the fish restaurant Barkas, they offer a large selection of delicious dishes at affordable prices. In addition to treats, guests can order their favorite drinks, the restaurant's wine list is also very diverse. Fans of a foamy drink will like the restaurant Birhouse (Beerhouse). Among the presented varieties of beer visitors will be able to find popular Czech, Belgian and German brands, and in addition to drinks order excellent treats. Among the signatory dishes of the restaurant are juicy steaks, grilled chicken wings, homemade sausages and pork ribs.

Vesuvio restaurant specializes in cooking Italian cuisine. Its beautifully decorated hall will be a great place for celebrations and banquets. On holidays, an interesting entertainment program is prepared for visitors. The restaurant East courtyard invites to try the best dishes of Arabic cuisine. The main "highlight" of the restaurant remains a rich selection of meat delicacies, a considerable part of the dishes are cooked on open fire. Visitors to the restaurant stay until late at night, in the evenings live music is always played for guests.

An original establishment is the restaurant Goodzone, which offers visitors, unique author's dishes. Each of the restaurant's refreshment is unique. Connoisseurs of modern cuisine will surely like to rest here. The restaurant Camelot specializes in cooking European cuisine. It can be recommended to vegetarians. The choice of all kinds of salads, vegetable stews and fruit desserts is simply magnificent. In the warm season, restaurant tables are served on the outdoor terrace by the fountain.

Restaurant Oliver also offers guests a wide selection of national and popular European dishes. Regular visitors especially note the attentive attitude of the staff and high-quality service.

Traditions & lifestyle
Colors of Dnepropetrovsk traditions, festivals, mentality and lifestyle
Traditions and customs of locals are very colorful and original. All national and family holidays here are held in observance of rites that remain relevant for many centuries. Locals are not strangers to the interests that are typical of most modern people, but they treat the traditions of their ancestors with special honor and respect. Like many years ago, locals believe in evil spirits and the power of amulets. To protect your house and loved ones from evil, it is customary to observe a lot of interesting traditions. In each house there is certainly a charm, which is made independently and stored away from prying eyes. If a person goes to an important and responsible event, you can

be sure that he also has a cherished amulet with him, which will certainly help in matters.

Family life is accompanied by interesting rites and rituals. Travelers who are lucky enough to attend a local wedding will have the opportunity to see colorful dance and music performances. At every wedding there are certainly funny games, entertainment and, of course, a rich celebratory table.

The birth of a child is the most important event for every married couple. The future mother tries to hide her condition from others as long as possible. According to one of the beliefs, the longer the surrounding people do not know about the coming of the baby, the easier will be the birth, and the child will certainly be born healthy. For the baby to grow strong and healthy, the first baptism must necessarily be with holy water. If a girl was born, then it is customary to add milk, honey and flowers to the baptismal font - then she will grow up to be a real beauty.

The most important for each family is a house in which order is always maintained and an overwhelming atmosphere of comfort prevails. Before building a house it is customary to perform a lot of complex rituals, then life in it will be happy and easy. Despite the fact that modern residents of Dnipropetrovsk live, in the main, apartments, all the traditions preserved from the ancestors are applicable to them. If the family moves into a new dwelling, then in honor of this important event they are sure to arrange a big holiday - Vydyhny. It is customary to invite many guests to a housewarming party and cover a rich table with refreshments. Guests, in turn, ought not to come empty-handed; landlords should definitely give memorable souvenirs.

One of the most favorite holidays for locals is Christmas. On the day of the holiday, colorful shopping tents with Christmas souvenirs and beautiful dishes appear on the streets of the city. The fact is that according to one of the traditions for Christmas, the housewives should buy new dishes, on which festive treats for guests will be served.

Tips for tourists
Preparing your trip to Dnepropetrovsk: advices & hints things to do and to obey
1. Locals are treated visitors are quite restrained and benevolent. If necessary, they can always ask the way to interesting attractions or ask other interesting questions.

2. The working hours of museums and other cultural institutions are best determined at the tourist office. Those who want to visit a local theater or go to music concert, best purchase tickets in advance. For some cultural events, ticket sales are completed in a few days.

3. The city is convenient to travel by bus, you can freely get to any area of interest on them. Taxis are best called on the phone or taken

at special parking lots, stopping a free car on the street can be quite difficult. The fare in a taxi depends on the firm and on the time of day, at night the tariff is higher than in the daytime.

4. You can rent a car in one of the many rental locations, the rental price depends on the specific brand of the car and can range from $30 to $200 per day. For rent, you will need an international driving license and a passport. The service may be refused to drivers who are younger than 21 years, as well as those who received the license less than two years ago.

5. In large restaurants, there is certainly a menu in English. Tipping is usually included in the bill; they rarely make up more than 10% of the ordered amount. In small restaurants and cafes you can also leave a tip, 5% of the bill amount will be enough.

6. In the city, it is very difficult to find a restaurant that is designed for vegetarians. At the same time, in almost every gastronomic institution visitors will be offered a rich selection of vegetable side dishes and salads, as well as delicious dishes from potatoes.

7. It is best to go to shops and markets with local currency. Some sellers accept payment in US dollars, but the exchange rate against the national currency will be extremely unprofitable. In most shopping centers you can pay by cashless settlement but you will need an international credit card for this.

8. Exchange of currency is best in banks, which accept visitors from Monday to Friday, from 9 am to 5 pm. Some banks can work until 19:00, and exchange offices usually close no earlier than 21:00.

9. A variety of charms and amulets are common souvenirs that visitors can buy in almost any souvenir shop. Sometimes they can be made in the form of interesting ornaments for home or jewelry, which will be an excellent memorable gift.

10. Travelers who stay at Dnepropetrovsk airport can get to the city center by tram number 1, this method will be the cheapest. The train station from the airport can be reached by bus number 109 or 60. Tourists also have the opportunity to take a taxi, but they will not be cheap.

11. In Dnepropetrovsk is the most large-scale bus station in Ukraine, which is worth a visit even for those who do not plan to go on a bus tour. Here there is a currency exchange office, as well as a timetable for city public transport.

12. For travelers who in addition to Dnepropetrovsk expect to visit the surrounding cities, it will be most convenient to travel by electric trains. Night bus tickets are also in demand, but this option will not be the best for long trips, especially in summer.

13. Dnepropetrovsk is a large-scale active city, and therefore congestion on its central highways has long been not uncommon. This

should be taken into account not only for those who prefer to travel by private car, but also for those who plan to use public transport services.

14. A few years ago, Dnepropetrovsk was a closed city, and today it is a permanent venue for major cultural events and festivals. Fans of event tourism should confirm the time of the holidays in advance, as the city's cultural calendar is updated and expanded annually.

15. The ideal time for a vacation with children will be summer, at this time the choice of interesting entertainment in Dnepropetrovsk is especially great. On city streets and in parks for children are equipped fine recreation areas with a lot of carousels and attractions.

16. Those who prefer to relax in a quiet environment should best visit Dnepropetrovsk in early autumn. At this time in the city reigns a very quiet atmosphere and the weather is excellent for active recreation and walks.

Donetsk

Guide to Donetsk

Sightseeing in Donetsk what to see. Complete travel guide
The city was founded in the 17th century when its territory was used as a Cossack settlement. The first metallurgic plant was opened here in the middle of the 19th century. It granted Donetsk the status of the industrial city. The main sight of the city is devoted to its industrial

prosperity. We are talking about Mertsalov Palm that was created in 1896 from a piece of rail. The original monument is acknowledged as a unique masterpiece; it has got many awards and today the monument adorns the entrance of the Mining Institute in Saint Petersburg. One of the Donetsk squares keeps the copy of the monument that was made according to the project of smith Sergei Kapruk in 1998.

One more amazing monument is devoted to a famous opera singer A.B. Solovyanenko. The monument is installed on the square in front of the National Academic Theater that also has the name of the great singer. Another wonderful monument has been installed to praise the founder of the city and is called "the monument of John James Hughes". In 1872 Hughes founded a small settlement called Yuzivka on the territory of the modern city. Tourists, who like old buildings, should visit the house of Hughes that still keeps many interesting and old items. In the house you will see wonderful paintings and furniture, drafts and important documents. John Lames Hughes has been the founder of one of the city's factories and a famous entrepreneur, so the house still has several folders with documents and projects. Today these papers are considered important museum's exhibits.

You should definitely visit Donetsk Regional Art Museum as this is one of the largest museums in Ukraine. The museum exhibits a collection of paintings; here often take place exhibitions devoted to modern art.

Local History Museum is also worth your attention. Its collection exceeds 120 thousands of priceless items.

The most interesting sight of Donetsk is the Pharmacy Museum Lache. At the end of the 19th century, a doctor from Belgium, Lache, moved to the city. He opened a pharmacy on the first floor of his house, which at that time, was one of the largest in the city. In this pharmacy, various medications were prepared and sold, and you could even buy cosmetic products in it. Despite the fact that over the years the historical building has changed its appearance several times, the internal setting of the pharmacy has remained virtually unchanged. Today, the museum houses an interesting collection of things one way or another, related to the pharmacy business.

There are many picturesque parks in the city, and even more symbolic monuments. A special place is the Park of Forged Figures. On its territory, there are real works of blacksmith's art. Absolutely all the sculptures presented on the territory of the park were forged by local blacksmiths. Here you can see figures of very different subjects. Among them there are miniature copies of world famous landmarks, and the symbolical signs of the Zodiac, as well as thematic figures, including those dedicated to football.

Donetsk has a beautiful botanical garden, which was founded in 1964. This garden is huge; its area is more than 260 hectares, and more than 5.5 thousand plants can be seen in it. During the walk, visitors to the garden can admire the beautiful ponds located on its territory. Also, several beautiful old buildings still remain in the garden. Many unique plants are kept in the greenhouse; you can admire them even in winter.

In Donetsk, many fine historical monuments of various periods, among which the spectacular House of Balfour, have been preserved. This magnificent house was built in 1889 for one of the wealthy local industrialists. At the end of the 19th century, the territory around the house was decorated with a luxurious garden. To this day, the beautiful garden has not been preserved, while the historic building and the surrounding buildings stay almost unchanged.

A bright architectural monument of the beginning of the 20th century is Gorelik's House. It also bears the name of its first owner - a wealthy merchant. During the revolutionary period, this historical building housed a printing house, and aftert, a radio center. A lot of interesting stories are connected with the historical building. According to one of them, Mayakovsky lived here for some time in his life and read poems from the balcony.

Family trip with kids

Family trip to Donetsk with children. Ideas on where to go with your child

Among the sights of Donetsk especially interesting for visiting with children, it is worth noting the Park Shcherbakova. It is one of the largest and most beautiful parks in the city, where in summer there are always lots of attractions and playgrounds for children. The park is ideal for walking, because there are many beautiful fountains and sculptures on its territory, and in summer, the park is decorated with luxurious flower beds. There is a Ferris wheel on which the whole family can ride and excellent cafes where one can try branded sweets.

Nature lovers should definitely look into the Donetsk Botanical Garden. It is covered, so is available for visiting at any time of the year. Here in the spacious pavilions, one can see exotic palm trees and a rich collection of cacti, incredibly beautiful flowers and the main inhabitants of the garden - beautiful butterflies. In the warm season, a beautiful landscape park is equipped on the adjacent territory of the garden, a walk along which adults and children will also enjoy.

A very special institution whose main visitors are also tourists and locals with children is the Donetsk Digital Planetarium. It is located in a beautiful modern building and offers visitors special educational programs, during which they can learn a lot of interesting things about the stars, the Milky Way and even the mysterious Mayan calendar, around which there are so many myths and mysteries. The main feature of the planetarium is the first-class digital equipment, which allows one to make a change of scenery as effective as possible. In the planetarium, interesting programs are conducted for children of various ages. It will be interesting to visit it, even with the kids.

For those who prefer active entertainment, it is certainly worth visiting the aquapark Aquasferra. This water park is indoors and is located in a beautiful modern building with a glass roof and walls. The choice of entertainment here is simply wide. The water park presents dozens of slides of various levels of difficulty, special pools for children, and recreation areas. The park has a café and a souvenir shop, and it will be pleasant and interesting to relax here at any time of the year.

Donetsk Aquarium is also worth a visit by the whole family. It is one of the oldest and most interesting aquariums in the country. In addition to fish and other inhabitants of the marine depths, it introduces visitors to the wonderful world of reptiles. The aquarium contains a rich collection of snakes. Its visitors will have the opportunity to stroke a python and even take a picture with it. Also, the zoo is equipped with a special cage for crocodiles. Many regular visitors come to the aquarium at a specially marked time to watch how the staff feed the crocodiles and other inhabitants.

Another amazing place worth visiting with children is the Park of Forged Figures. It is a large and beautiful park, which besides trees, is decorated with very original forged sculptures. Among them, one can see copies of world famous landmarks, as well as unusual abstract figures and even figures of fairy-tale characters familiar to all from childhood. In this park, one can take pictures with a miniature Tower of Pisa or against the backdrop of figures of formidable heroes who rise from the ground, while football fans can be photographed against the backdrop of a huge UEFA Cup. The park is very beautiful and well maintained; a walk along it will be pleasant and interesting at any time of the year.

Culture: sights to visit

Culture of Donetsk. Places to visit old town, temples, theaters, museums and palaces

Start your acquaintance with the landmarks of the city with a stroll in the Forged Figures Park that is located not far from the city council building. It is a beautiful and large park with numerous interesting and attractive monuments and sculptures that were created by best artisans of Donbas. The park has become a regular venue for the annual smithcraft festival. The sculptures made during this festival then become the main decorations of the park, so the number of exhibits only increases every year.

Children will also find it very interesting to visit this park, mostly because there is "Glade of fairy tales" in its territory. All figures of famous and most loved fairytale characters are installed in this part of the park. Pushkin Boulevard remains one of the most popular destinations for tourists. There are many interesting buildings and charming shops along the boulevard. This is also the location of the famous Mertsalov's Palm that has become the main symbol of the city. The elegant sculpture of a palm is installed in the center of the boulevard. By the way, it is a precise copy of the sculpture that is exhibited in one of Saint Petersburg's museums.

Among the most notable landmarks located not far from the boulevard, it is important to mention the city hall building and the Donetsk Museum of Local History that regularly hosts interesting cultural events. When describing other notable landmarks of Donetsk, it is important to mention Tsar Cannon that is located on the square in front of the city council building. The gorgeous monument made of cast iron was installed in 2001. It is a precise copy of the Tsar Cannon installed in Moscow. The length of the cannon's barrel exceeds 5 meters, and its weight is more than 20 tons.

Guests of the city simply cannot leave Donetsk until they visit the Opera Theater that is open in a gorgeous building that dates back to the middle of the 20th century. The repertoire of the theater includes plays that are not available in any other theater of the country. It would also be a mistake not to mention Central Scherbakov Park of Culture and Leisure. It is decorated with interesting sculptures and monuments. There are also several interesting attractions that children are usually very happy to visit. When taking a stroll in the park, vacationers can reach the waterfront that has become one of the most favorite destinations for romantic couples.

Among cultural venues of the city, the Donetsk Railway Museum definitely deserves a mention. This museum is open in the building of the railway station. An old railway is one of the main treasures of the museum. Visitors can admire retro trains and explore old carriages from the inside.

Attractions & nightlife

City break in Donetsk. Active leisure ideas for Donetsk attractions, recreation and nightlife

Besides strolls to interesting historical landmarks and observation of priceless collections in local museums, guests of Donetsk have an opportunity to visit numerous entertainment venues. There are suitable establishments for music fans, shopaholics, and families that visit the city with their children. Vacationers will find it interesting to visit the picturesque Botanic Garden that is present in the list of the largest and most beautiful botanic gardens in Europe. Its collection features more than 8 thousands of different plants. The garden was founded in 1964. It is open all year round because there is a quality greenhouse in the territory of the complex.

The Nemo Dolphinarium accepts visitors all year round. It is a great place for the whole family. Visitors are welcome to swim with dolphins in the swimming pool, watch fabulous shows, and find out a lot of interesting information about the friendliest marine creatures. In addition to daytime performances, there are no less interesting night shows.

Fans of nighttime entertainment will find it very interesting to attend Chicago that regularly hosts interesting dancing and music performances. The club also has an amazing bar where visitors can order not only various beverages and unusual cocktails but also popular European and Asian cuisine dishes. X-Bar is a no less wonderful venue. Skilled barmen are always ready to impress their guests with the most exotic and trendiest cocktails. Energetic parties in this bar have become a legend, so no wonder why it is so popular. Seventh Heaven is a one more famous nightclub that regularly hosts all kinds of music events, various presentations, and celebrations.

Hollywood nightclub is no less attractive. By the way, one of the best national cuisine restaurants in Donetsk is open in this club. Beer fans will genuinely enjoy spending an evening in Opera Club. The club's bar offers the best beer types and a broad range of appetizers and snacks. Guests of Opera Club can sit in the main hall and watch an interesting entertainment program or decide to relax in a more intimate setting in the so-called "pub". Finally, all fans of karaoke will be amazed by Tribune Lounge Club. Besides its main attraction, the club regularly hosts colorful parties and pampers its guests with a great choice of delicacies.

Horse excursions are very popular with active recreation fans. It is a very exciting pastime that is equally appealing to adults and children. The most popular equestrian clubs in the region are the following:

Tatersal and Jaguar. Tourists may also find it interesting to watch equestrian shows there is Donbass Equicentre for that purpose in the city of a million roses (that is a popular informal name of Donetsk). Donbass Equicentre regularly hosts international competitions and events, so tourists are recommended to check the schedule of upcoming events in advance. Needless to say, it is a wonderful pastime that is very popular with people of different age groups.

Motuzkovyy Park Len v Pen is a great destination for a family day out. Children are particularly happy to spend a day at the rope park. They energetically explore the area and have fun trying numerous interesting attractions. As there are many security devices, visitors don't need to be extra cautious and worry about safety measures. Aquasferra Aqua Park is one more place that kids will be simply happy to visit. Many parents gift a visit to this aquatic center as a birthday present and make a fantastic party there. There are many slides and different attractions, so children will have plenty of space to relax and have fun.

Children's Railway of Priklonskiy offers a very interesting activity to all children. They can try such adult professions as ticket check-man and train host. A visit to the children's railway will please both kids and their parents. Donetsk Aquarium is one more amazing place that is perfectly suitable for the whole family. Crocodile and python have become true symbols of this place. Vacationers in a mood for some bowling will hardly find a better place than Virus Center. In case there is a wish to raise the adrenaline level, consider visiting an escape room. In Donetsk, a company with the simple name Escape offers this entertainment to locals and guests of the city.

Tourists wishing to watch the newest films can easily do that in Donetsk. There are several modern cinemas in the city, with House of Cinema "Shevchenko", Multiplex, and Kinocult being the most popular. Travelers, who enjoy watching sports competitions, are always welcome to watch different games that regularly take place in Donbas Arena or Druzhba Arena. These are quite unique stadiums that are interesting to visit. The only thing that tourists need to do is to check the schedule of upcoming events. The city also has suitable venues for people who want to watch theatrical plays, opera or listen to classical music. Donetsk State Academic Opera and Ballet Theatre named after A. Solovyanenko and Donets'ka Derzhavna Akademichna Filarmoniya offer all these to their visitors.

The city of a million roses is famous not only for its manufacturing industry and countless roses planted in endless flowerbeds but also for its numerous interesting landmarks that have become legendary among both locals and guests of Donetsk. For example, it is believed that Joseph Kobzon Monument brings good luck to everyone who touches its right hand. Newlyweds in Donetsk also have an interesting tradition. They go to Central Scherbakov Park of Culture and Leisure and hang a lock on the bridge. After that, they throw the key to the water. This ritual is aimed to bring a happy life to the new family. Students are traditionally the most superstitious people. There is a monument of a student near the economy and law faculty of Donetsk National University. Students believe that if they touch this monument, they will pass exams with good marks.

Tourists wishing to learn more about local traditions and culture will also enjoy their stay in Donetsk. For that purpose, consider visiting such museums as Donetsk regional museum of local history that is a perfect destination for everyone who wants to get acquainted with the history of the region. Football fans will be excited to find out that there is a museum dedicated to football in Donetsk - FC Shakhtar Museum. Local people also do not forget about lessons of the biggest war in the history of humanity. The local Museum of the Great Patriotic War is dedicated to this theme. All fans of art are recommended to check the Art Donbas Gallery and Paduano Arte salon.

Cuisine & restaurants

Cuisine of Donetsk for gourmets. Places for dinner best restaurants
Thanks to a large number of luxurious restaurants and charming cafes, Donetsk is ready to please even most discerning foodies. Guests of the city should definitely visit local cafes and restaurants that please their visitors not only with delicious food but also with an interesting

entertaining program. Stylish and eye-catching, Bruderschaft is famous as one of the best restaurants in the city. In the menu of this dining establishment, visitors will find the most popular Italian, French, Hungarian, German, and Baltic dishes. It will be hard to find such a broad range of culinary masterpieces in any other restaurant in Donetsk. Bruderschaft is also perfectly suitable for events and celebrations. Friendly and attentive staff will help to organize any holiday.

For a family visit, Family Club is, perhaps, the most suitable. This restaurant complex is located in Central Scherbakov Park of Culture and Leisure, and it offers a range of popular national dishes that are available at very attractive prices. Family Club's visitors are welcome to relax in a beautiful hall or choose to stay outdoors and enjoy the fresh air on a spacious terrace. Besides an elegant restaurant, there is a beautiful café with a great choice of desserts, appetizers, and beverages.

In Donetsk, there is a restaurant that specializes in English cuisine - Foggy Albion. The design of this restaurant is reminiscent of a classic British castle. Massive furniture made of rare sorts of wood, gorgeous chandeliers, and premium textiles make this restaurant look like an elegant banquet hall from the past. There is also an attractive bar at Foggy Albion. It offers many interesting cocktails and beverages. In addition to traditional English food, guests of this restaurant are welcome to try various pastries and home cuisine dishes. Fans of Italian food, in their turn, will be in love with Pasta Project. As one can easily guess from the name, pasta is the main specialty of this restaurant. At Pasta Project, guests are welcome to try several dozen types of this ever-popular Italian dish, and each culinary masterpiece is distinguished by an inimitable, unforgettable taste. The restaurant has a rich wine list because it is simply impossible to imagine an Italian style dinner without a glass of fragrant wine.

All fans of Mediterranean cuisine also have a must-visit restaurant in Donetsk - Piu Gusto. This dining establishment usually has a range of interesting offers to its guests. For example, visitors are welcome to try oysters cooked in accordance with the signature recipe, enjoy piquant Sicilian dishes, and numerous signature fish dishes. Fans of exotic food will be excited to try stingray soup and grilled flounder.

The traditional cuisine that many Donetsk restaurants specialize in is very diverse. Different first-course dishes are very popular in the region. Besides that, there are many interesting dishes with vegetables and meat. Pork fat or Salo remains one of the main symbols of the national cuisine. Among the first course dishes, Borsch is the number one choice. This soup has beetroot as its main ingredient. The vegetable adds a deep red color to the dish, thanks to which it is not possible to mistake Borsch for any other soup.

Cabbage soup is a no less popular local dish. Cabbage is the main ingredient of this soup, and both raw and fermented forms of cabbage are accepted. Restaurants specializing in the national cuisine also offer Rassolnik. This is a traditional soup with pickled cucumbers that add a peculiar taste.

The choice of second-course dishes in Donetsk restaurants is no less amazing. Tourists, who do not know what to order, should try Varenyky. Similar filled dumplings are present in many cuisines of the world, but only in the local cuisine Varenyky remain important everyday food. They can come with savory or sweet fillings, so certain types of Varenyky can easily replace a dessert. Potatoes, cabbage, mushrooms, meat, other seasonal fruit and vegetables the choice of fillings for Varenyky is incredibly diverse.

Halusky are a very interesting local specialty. These are small pieces of boiled dough that can be served either as the main dish or as a garnish. As a rule, Halusky are usually served with sour cream. There are also soups with this food. A real surprise awaits all fans of meat delicacies in local restaurants specializing in the national cuisine. They can try Buzhenina with the traditional bread and bacon crisps pieces of Salo or fatty meat roasted until they become crispy.

Zrazy is a very popular local dish that can easily vary in shape and size. Sometimes, Zrazy look like small cutlets stuffed with vegetables or mushrooms, and sometimes it can be a true meat roll. When it is dessert time, Donetsk restaurants usually offer all kinds of pastries. Local people like Nalesniki, small pancakes with different fillings. Besides that, tourists usually like Syrniki, a special pastry with cottage cheese. There is also an interesting sweet pastry with potato being its main ingredient Deruny. Many local restaurants serve sour cream in addition to many sweet pastries.

Traditions & lifestyle

Colors of Donetsk traditions, festivals, mentality and lifestyle
Residents of the city of a million roses (this is a popular way to call Donetsk because there is virtually a countless number of this flower in the city) are hospitable, friendly, and charming people. If one manages to win their trust, they can always rely on locals. Donetsk residents are true friends who are always ready to help, no matter how hard it can be. That said, despite the fact that local people might look reserved at a glance, tourists shouldn't be afraid to ask them to help.

When talking to locals, it is better not to touch such theme as politics. Indigenous people are proud of their independence, and there is nothing bad in that. However, if their opinion doesn't coincide with the opinion of their opponent, that can become a reason for an argument. Here it is important to mention that locals are quite passionate when defending their ideas. And this quality, indeed, deserves praise. It is safe to say that locals will fight for their beliefs until the end and get the job done no matter what. Family, relatives, and close friends are the biggest treasure for local people and they are ready to protect the ones they love.

It is important to mention the multinationality of the city. This fact has found reflection in the local culture and cuisine. For example, such Ukrainian cuisine dishes as borsch, varenyky, salo (in any form roasted, boiled, salted, smoked, stewed, and even raw), halusky, and syrniki are particularly popular in the region. When mixed with Russian cuisine, local culinary traditions become particularly appealing. Dumplings and cabbage (stewed or fermented) are also very popular, as well as dishes with potato, mushrooms, and berries.

Festivals, which take place in Donetsk, are bright and colorful events that traditionally attract numerous guests. Donbas Xtreme Fest is, for sure, one of the most unusual events in the festival life of the city. As a rule, the event takes place at the end of May. It is an interesting open-air festival that is dedicated to active recreation and extreme sports (alpinism, zip line, water-based activities, yoga, hang gliding, paintball, Frisbee). Besides that, visitors are welcome to attend various music concerts and listen to different music styles, including French chanson and popular hits from the 80s of the previous century. The fest is also a great way to try local delicacies. The event takes place in Zuyivs'kyy Rehional'nyy Landshaftnyy Park that is very comfortable for such occasions.

TerriCON is one more interesting festival in Donetsk. As one can guess by the name, this event is dedicated to comics, pop culture, and cosplays. During the festival, visitors can attend costume contests and meet-and-greets with famous people in the cosplay scene. Music plays non-stop, adding to the cheering mood of everyone present for fans of villains and superheroes and, of course, for cosplayers. It is a true holiday because people with the same passion are able to meet and share their emotions. The festival takes place in the middle of September.

The beginning of July marks the start of one more notable event in the city of a million roses. It is the time for Lava Fest, one of the best festivals in the region that is dedicated to the hip-hop culture. Among headliners of the festival, there are always famous bands and performers. The event takes place on Metalurh Stadium. The main aim of the festival is to entertain people and make sure that no one feels bored during Lava Fest. To tell the truth, the event succeeds in that it becomes so hot during the festival that this energy busts like during a volcano explosion. That is the reason why the event was named Lava Fest.

Jazz is popular in Donetsk, and the jazz festival that takes place in the city at the beginning of December is another proof of that. The event is called DoDj (meaning Donetsk Jazz) and takes place in the State Academic Opera and Ballet Theatre. Among headliners of the event, there are famous jazz and blues musicians not only from Ukraine but also from other countries, including Europe. During the festival, young performers are welcome to participate in an interesting contest called DoDj Junior. This is not the only event dedicated to jazz in Donetsk. There is one more festival, Jazz Forum, that takes place in Derzhavna Akademichna Filarmoniya in the middle of March. During this event, visitors can listen to musicians from the European Union, the United States, and Russia.

The end of November is a great time for all guests of Donetsk as they are welcome to attend a large event dedicated to food, namely, the National Food Festival. Visitors can try different cuisines of the world, including Kazakh, Uzbek, Russian, Armenian, and, of course, Ukrainian. Samsa, Dolma, Kebab, Halusky, Pampushky, marinades, and Chebureki visitors are welcome to try all these and more at the venue of the festival. By the way, the food festival takes place in the Forged Figures Park. The atmosphere that reigns in this park is nothing but fantastic. It makes even complete strangers feel like friends who have known each other for ages. Besides cuisine related activities, the schedule of the festival includes music and dancing performances.

Art Alternative is one more interesting event that takes place in Donetsk at the beginning of April. It is dedicated to experimental dramatic art. This is a multifaceted festival, during which visitors have a unique opportunity to watch and listen to various performances, attend various exhibitions, and participate in interesting master-classes held by professionals who visit this popular event. Besides that, guests of the festival can enjoy a fascinating music program. The event changes its location every year. It can take place in Donetsk Performing Arts Theater, Regional Academic Puppet Theatre, Academical Russian Theatre for Young Spectator or, for example, in Chicago nightclub. Travelers need to check the venue in advance prior to their visit to the city of a million roses.

One more popular theatre-related event in the city has a simple name Theatre Donbas. This festival takes place in Donetsk National Academic Ukrainian Musical and Drama Theatre at the end of March. During this event, visitors have an opportunity to see the best new plays and performances. One more grandiose event takes place in the city of a million roses approximately at the same time. This is S. Prokofiev's Native Land music festival and the international competition for young pianists. As one can guess from the name, this is a classical music festival that also has an aim of uniting peoples of Donbas. The popular music event takes place in Prokofiev's Donetsk State Music Academy. Among participants of the festival, there are musicians from different countries of the world.

Shopping in Donetsk

Shopping in Donetsk authentic goods, best outlets, malls and boutiques

In the very heart of Donetsk is located Green Plaza shopping and entertainment center. It is one of the most beautiful and visited in the city. In it, there're shops of popular European brands, nice pavilions with goods for the house and specialized shops with goods for children. The center has a luxurious appearance. Natural plants and flowers are arranged everywhere, as well as recreation areas with benches and playgrounds for children.

On the central street of Donetsk, Donetsk City trading center is located, which offers its visitors excellent conditions for shopping. You can go round here in search of new clothes, visit perfumery stores, jewelry salons, and even buy interesting gifts for relatives. There are excellent conditions for not only shopping but for entertainment, as well.

White Swan complex is one more perfect place to make purchases. It is located in the building of a historic department store, whose opening was held in 1965. For many years, local residents went here to buy new clothes and shoes. Nowadays, clothes of the most popular international brands are available here.

Those who like to shop in a stylish modern setting, will appreciate Decor Donbass. Its opening took place in 2007. The area of the four-storey shopping center is 70000 sq. m. It includes shops of various specialization, including dozens of clothing and accessories stores, several large sports shops, and pavilions with electronics. You can walk around this shopping center all day long complementing shopping with leisure in cozy cafes.

Central Department Store is a real attraction of Donetsk. Its opening was held in 1937. Initially, only the most upscale and prestigious stores were opened in it. The department store was the largest and most visited one in the city. Over the war years, the building of the department store was partially destroyed, but after the war, it was quickly restored. Nowadays, it is one of the oldest in the city. Currently, TSUM houses a lot of elite stores. It will definitely appeal to amateurs of designer things.

Those who avoid crowded and noisy places, should go to Aquarelle trading center. It is quite small, nevertheless, it presents shops of various categories. Here, you'll find clothes of different stylistic trends, and choose new accessories and perfumery. There are excellent stores here, where they sell quality home textiles, gift and souvenir products.

You will find many excellent jewelry stores in Donetsk. Zarina store is one of the best in its category. This jewelry house is one of the oldest in the country. All of its products are of the highest quality and exclusivity. It offers exclusive jewelry that wealthy and demanding customers can afford. Frugal visitors will also choose excellent items at affordable prices.

Those who want to bring unusual souvenirs from Donetsk, should come by Indo-China store. They sell incredibly interesting hand-made articles and accessories from China, Tibet, India, and other Asian countries. Here, you can choose souvenirs for all tastes. Aspiring chefs have a large choice of Asian spices, adherents of Feng Shui may choose new interesting talismans and decorations for the house.

Wealthy tourists usually prefer Presents store. They can choose elite gifts and souvenirs from around the world. In this store, they sell crystal and porcelain dishes from the best world manufacturers, as well as gift versions of chess and stylish ornaments for the office. This store is sure to please men since it offers weapons collections, stylish canes and various collectibles that will not leave them indifferent.

Feodosiya

Guide to Feodosiya

Sightseeing in Feodosiya what to see. Complete travel guide
The history of Feodosia goes back over 25 centuries. It is one of the oldest towns in the world. Besides the unique nature, the main value of the enchanting Crimean town is historical monuments. In the surroundings of Feodosia, there are several large archaeological areas that everyone can visit. The enchanting city provides its guests with a wide choice of activities. The acquaintance with unique historical attractions, walking along picturesque places, beach recreation, hiking the resort provides perfect conditions for family recreation.

Feodosia is the homeland of the world-famous artist, I. K. Aivazovsky who was inspired by wonderful sea landscapes. In the town, there is an excellent art gallery that is dedicated to the artist's art and houses the rich collection of his masterpieces.

In Feodosia, there are also several upscale wellness centers that will be perfect places for tourists wanting to improve their health. The enchanting old town is well-developed from a tourist point of view. When walking, travelers can see attractive restaurants, cafes, interesting gift shops and stalls where you can buy a lot of tasty sweets and house wine. In the town, there are no big entertainment venues but its picturesque streets always have quite a lively atmosphere.

The main features of the town are plenty of beautiful squares, near which you can see unique monuments of cultural heritage. The parks and squares of Feodosia will impress you with their well-groomed appearance and thoughtful design. The town was damaged significantly in wartime. Most of the historical sites of Feodosia were destroyed. Due to the locals' effort, the part of the historical heritage was restored, so the sightseeing program offered to tourists can't be called modest. Ancient mansions and villas, outstanding cult constructions and the ruins of old fortresses, symbolic monuments and museums it is just impossible to explore all these sites in one day.

Feodosia will impress fans of different kinds of sport. It is a harmonious and beautiful Crimean resort.

In the surroundings of Feodosia, there are several beautiful medieval fortresses. The most famous of them is the Genoese Fortress Kafa. It was built in the 14th century. Originally, the fortress was a big architectural complex. It included several large palaces, administrative buildings, a bishop's residence, and different outbuildings. By the 19th century, the fortress had lost its original strategic status and been almost destroyed. Only several medieval towers, some walls, old churches, and the bathhouse have survived to this day.

Some of the medieval defensive constructions are located right on the territory of the city. One of them is the Tower of St. Constantine. It was built in 1382 to protect the coastal zone from conquerors. In the late 15th century, the tower was conquered by Ottoman conquerors and partially rebuilt. The historical value of the construction was recognized at the beginning of the 20th century. It was reconstructed completely at that time.

Another beautiful architectural monument is Cottage Stamboli. It was built for the local wealthy merchant in 1914. As many other luxurious constructions, the cottage was nationalized after the Revolution of 1917. Then, it served as a sanatorium. In wartime, the hospital that had been open for many years was founded here. In the middle of the

20th century, the historic building served as a restaurant. There is the Museum of Underwater Archeology opened in 2013.

The must-see is the Local History Museum of Feodosia. Its collection started being formed at the beginning of the 19th century. In 1811, the Museum of Antiques was opened in the city. Its exhibits have become a core of the collection of the future local history museum. Ivan Konstantinovich Aivazovsky contributed much to the museum development. The first separate building was built at his expense. Consequently, the museum has changed its location several times, as its collection has been rapidly broadened. Today, it occupies the beautiful estate built in the period between the 19th and 20th centuries. The museum houses the collection of interesting archeological artifacts that have been found when the surroundings of Feodosia were explored.

Hurzuf

Guide to Hurzuf

Sightseeing in Hurzuf what to see. Complete travel guide
Gurzuf - one of the popular Crimean resorts, where every summer thousands of tourists come. The average annual air temperature here is exactly the same as in Nice, but precipitation falls, on the contrary, lesser than on the Cote d'Azur. The name of the village comes from the Latin word "Urzus", which means "bear". This is one of the most

charming villages of the Crimean coast, which was literally created for a serene leisure.

The resort is famous for its unique nature; in the heart of Gurzuf there is the Genoese rock and the Chaliapin rock, and in the bay waters the mysterious cliffs of Adalara rise. The first settlements on the territory of the modern city appeared more than 40 thousand years ago. On the Genoese rock, the ruins of the fortress of Gorzuvita, which was built during the reign of the Byzantine emperor Justinian, were preserved till our times. It is here that the most famous children's camp of the former Soviet Union "Artek", which was founded in 1925, is located.

Semi-ring mountains, towering 1.5 kilometers above sea level, protect Gurzuf from cold northern winds, and from the east the village is protected by Bear Mountain. On this territory in certain periods of history lived Taurians and Goths, a large ancient settlement was located here, and even a slab with an inscription in the ancient Greek language was preserved. In the 12th century, Gurzuf, then called Gorura, was a quite large and well fortified trade city. A significant part of the fortification was built when the Genoese were in control of it. In 1475, the Crimean Khanate, in whose territory the settlement was located, fell into a vassal dependence on Turkey, and the Ottomans marked out their military garrison here. After the end of the Russian-Turkish war, these lands were relegated to the Russian Empire.

The very first aristocrat seriously interested in these lands was Governor General Richelieu, who bought a piece of land and built a house with office buildings on it. After 10 years, it was bought by Governor General Vorontsov, but Gurzuf became a real benefactor of a large industrialist, Gubonin. It was he who revived the city, built several hotels, restaurants, electricity and landscaped park. At the end of the XIX century Gurzuf was one of the most comfortable resorts of the coast. Now Gurzuf is a modern resort with developed infrastructure, a wonderful coastline and quality clinics. It is with pleasure that tourists who want to visit the places that once attracted Pushkin, Chekhov and Mayakovsky, come here to relax.

The guests of the resort will have an opportunity to combine their favorite beach entertainments with an exciting tour program. In the city, there are many preserved beautiful historical constructions, including the fascinating Suuk Su Palace. It was built in the early 20th century. The initiators of its construction were the engineer Berezin and his wife. Under their guidance, a lot of beautiful architectural complexes, gardens and parks appeared on the territory of the resort. Now, the palace is located on the territory of one of the wonderful parks and considered as a vivid example of the Renaissance style.

In 2007, the Assumption Cathedral was built. The first church at its site was built several hundred years ago. In 1935, it was completely destroyed. The military sanatorium was constructed at its site. Not so long ago, the city government decided to restore this old church. It was rebuilt in accordance with all the traditions of the Russian and Byzantium style. Near the temple, there is the beautiful park where you can walk along branched acacias and cypresses.

The interesting culture center is the House of the famous Russian writer A. Chekhov. At the beginning of the 20th century, he bought a small cottage in Gurzuf. It is a miracle that the building was preserved in a period of the Second World War. In1963, it came under the Union of Artists. In the historical building, the museum dedicated to the writers' work was opened. Its collection includes Chekhov's writings, his personal belongings, pieces of antique furniture, and pieces of art.

Another interesting place is the old cottage of the famous artist K. Korovin. Now, this historic building serves as a themed museum dedicated to life and art of the former famous owner. In his cottage, the artist often held soirees that a lot of eminent people attended. I. Repin, F. Shalyapin, and A. Gorky often visited this house. The present collection of the museum is presented in 14 spacious rooms. The museum is surrounded by the big garden where you can admire not only exotic plants, but also old sculptures.

Culture: sights to visit
Culture of Hurzuf. Places to visit old town, temples, theaters, museums and palaces

A small picturesque resort is a place of a number of outstanding sights, therefore, holidaymakers have the opportunity to make a worthy excursion program. Since ancient times, Gurzuf has attracted creative personalities. Hundreds of years ago, literary figures and artists came here in search of inspiration. An important historical symbol of the resort is the house Richelieu - a beautiful manor of the early 19th century, which today is the location of the "A.C. Pushkin Museum". It was in this estate that Pushkin lived during his visit to Gurzuf. It is worth noting that to this day the building has remained practically unchanged, it is located on the territory of the beautiful Gurzuf Park. Annually on June 6 - the birthday of A.C. Pushkin - a beautiful literary holiday is held here.

House-Museum of A.P. Chekhov also deserves the attention of travelers interested in history and Russian literature. The place of its location was a small white cottage, which the locals call "Belaya Dacha". Chekhov was sent to Gurzuf in 1898 on the advice of doctors. The writer spent the last years of his life here. The museum was converted into a historical building in 1921. Thanks to the efforts of locals during the war, it was possible to preserve the priceless collection, so contemporaries have a unique opportunity to see Chekhov's personal belongings and manuscripts.

Fans of painting will be more interested in "K.A. Korovin's dacha", a famous artist of the early 20th century. His dacha, built in 1910, the artist called "Salammbo", and this name it still wears even now. During the Soviet era, the dacha was converted into a recreation center, and right after the war, in 1947, an art center was opened here. At present, "Salammbo" is a permanent venue for interesting art exhibitions.

There are outstanding architectural monuments in the resort, the history of which is also very interesting. Among them is the beautiful "Suuk-Su palace", the construction of which took place in the early 20th century on the initiative and under the leadership of the famous engineer V.I. Berezina. The beautiful palace was originally built as an apartment house. It was planned to found a hotel, as well as the first casino in the village here. The construction of the resort was finally completed by 1913; he won many honorable awards and was a favorite resting place for many outstanding personalities. In 1936 the beautiful palace was transferred to the children's complex "Artek".

Attractions & nightlife

City break in Hurzuf. Active leisure ideas for Hurzuf attractions, recreation and nightlife
Gurzuf Valley is incredibly beautiful. Here there is very clean air and exotic vegetation, which makes this area attractive in the eyes of environmental tourists and ordinary lovers of recreation in picturesque places. An original symbol of Gurzuf can be considered to be the cliff-twins Adalara and Mount Ayu-Dag. At the foot of this

mountain is the famous children's camp "Artek". The rest of the strip is occupied by popular sanatoria, including "Pushkino" and "Gurzufsky".

A separate attraction of the resort village is the embankment, which is ideal for leisurely walks. At the height of the tourist season on the waterfront there is always a lively atmosphere, the guests of the resort come here to admire the coast and buy memorable gifts. On the waterfront are the most popular restaurants and bars where you can dine, dance, listen to music or just sit on the terrace while admiring the sea. There are a lot of bars and discos in the resort, and every institution tries to attract visitors with a special entertainment program.

The main value of the famous Crimean resort was and remains beaches, the most popular among which is the "Artekovskiy", or, as it is more often called now, "Gurovsky Kamny". The beach will appeal to those who prefer a "wild" holiday. At the height of the tourist season in remote parts of the beach, tourists set up tents and spend the night at the very shore of the sea. There are also equipped beaches in the resort, which, in addition to standard equipment, can offer tourists a lot of interesting entertainment.

The village itself is very small; you can get around it all in just a couple of hours. The winding streets of the village are ideal for hiking, during which you can find a lot of interesting shopping tents and cozy places for recreation. An important feature of the resort is the abundance of artists who are located directly on the city streets and write local landscapes. Their work is in demand among holidaymakers. In Gurzuf you can order an excellent portrait or picture. You can walk around the beautiful park of the sanatorium "Gurzufsky" as much as you like, it is considered the most picturesque park of the South Coast. The park was decorated with ancient trees and beautiful fountains, this is one of the most romantic and quiet places in the resort. People of different ages and preferences will like to rest in a cozy and picturesque village.

Cuisine & restaurants

Cuisine of Hurzuf for gourmets. Places for dinner best restaurants
Representatives of different nationalities live in Gurzuf, and therefore the cuisine here is very diverse. After the conquest of the Crimean peninsula by the Russian Empire, Russian peasants moved here who then introduced the local population to traditional Russian dishes. Okroshka, borsch and pancakes are still very popular dishes, offered in many restaurants of the resort. Of course, the basis of local cookery is the dishes of Ukrainian cuisine; restaurants of this direction are the most common.

Among the classic Ukrainian dishes is popular aromatic and rich borsch with lard or dumplings, one plate of this hearty dish can satisfy you all day. Local chefs prepare a lot of interesting culinary masterpieces from meat and poultry. In each national restaurant guests are offered "vareniki" with cherries and elegant sweet pies.

There is also a lot of ethnic Crimean Tatars in Gurzuf, whose cuisine somewhat resembles the Mediterranean one. The basis of their cooking is meat dishes, for the preparation of which pork is mainly used. One of the most popular Tatar dishes is Sarma - small stuffed golubets with meat, wrapped in grape leaves, specially soaked and pickled. To supplement this dish is best with a light semi-dry wine, which in Gurzuf is an incredibly popular drink.

Uzbek restaurants are also popular in the resort, where you can try excellent pilaf, cooked according to the classic recipes of manta and samsa, as well as a juicy shish kebab. The Greeks also influenced the formation of Gurzuf's culinary traditions, and therefore in many cafes visitors are offered a classic Greek salad and cheese assortment, the ideal addition to these dishes will be local wine.

An attractive modern resort is not devoid of the fast food restaurants that are familiar to many travelers. Distributed here and a variety of cheburek house, which has long been chosen by adherents of budgetary vacation. On the way to the beach you can find a lot of traders who offer fresh homemade cakes and wine, it enjoys incredible popularity among travelers.

Tips for tourists

Preparing your trip to Hurzuf: advices & hints things to do and to obey

1. Guests of Gurzuf have an excellent opportunity to visit Simferopol, with which the resort is connected by regular trolleybus service. The nearest resort villages can easily be reached by fixed-route taxis; guests can use the services of an ordinary taxi at any time.

2. There are not many gastronomic institutions in Gurzuf, most of them are concentrated on the embankment and are oriented, first of all, to tourists. Local restaurants and cafes will pleasantly surprise guests with affordable prices, and even more economical tourists will like the tents near the beach with baked goods and soft drinks.

3. For those who prefer to cook their own food during the holidays, it is best to go for products in one of two local markets. Here local people buy food; the choice of goods in the market is simply excellent.

4. Fans of beach holidays should take into account that not all local beaches are free. Some parts of the coast belong to local sanatoriums; you can rest on such beaches only at an additional cost. Those who do not like to rest in noisy and crowded places will like paid beaches.

5. One of the main values of the resort is its unique nature. On the territory of some nature reserves, you can walk only accompanied by a guide, whose advice and recommendations should be strictly followed. Resting in the city parks, you need to keep clean, and you can only be on a picnic in specially designated places.

6. The most popular souvenirs for guests of the resort are paintings with images of natural attractions, crafts and ornaments from shells, as well as muscatel wine. Of special value is homemade wine, it should be chosen with great care. Honest salesmen always offer before buying, to try out the wine.

7. In Gurzuf, vacationers are presented with a decent choice of hotels and guesthouses for every taste and purse. Local hospitality facilities are distinguished by very attractive prices. Even in hotels of the highest category you can rent a luxurious room at a price characteristic of medium-priced hotels.

8. The sanatorium of Gurzuf deserves special attention. They are recommended to visit not only those who have expressed health problems, but also those who want to relax in a calm and secluded setting. Guests of local sanatoriums are guaranteed an upscale vacation and a lot of entertainment.

Kerch

Guide to Kerch
Sightseeing in Kerch what to see. Complete travel guide
Kerch is considered the most ancient city of Ukraine. It is in the east of the Crimean peninsula, right on the slopes of the ancient Greek Bosporus Cimmeria, which now bears the modern name of the Kerch Strait. The history of the city totals more than 2.5 thousand years and

probably, because of this, Kerch is considered one of the most multinational cities of the Crimea. The history of the city began with the founding of an ordinary Greek colony, which was called Panticapaeum. The city developed rapidly, and a lot of different settlements and necropolises arose around it, which are still important sights of Kerch.

More than a thousand burial mounds were preserved here, the most famous of which are: Golden, Royal, Yuz-Oba and Melek-Chesmensky. Literally, through several centuries the powerful Panticapaeum and several other cities united in the Bosporan kingdom, the capital of which became Panticapaeum. The kingdom lasted almost a thousand years. Many times these lands fell under the authority of the Roman Empire, but it also happened that the state became independent for several centuries.

Already in the 5th century the tribes of the barbarians finally established their dominion in these territories. The cities were destroyed, the local people were taken into slavery and chaos and devastation reigned in the once-fertile lands. The era of rebirth began after these lands fell under the rule of Byzantium, which restored the ancient city. True, the peaceful existence did not last long. After the emergence of Kievan Rus, the Slavic tribes were interested in these areas, and called it the ancient city of Korchev.

After bloody battles Korchev became one of the key cities of the Tmutarakan principality, which is part of Russia. In the XIV century Genoese came to these lands, and they built a large seaport with shore fortifications. The rule of the Genoese lasted only a hundred years, after which the city was captured by the Turks. Cherzeti, as Kerch was called in those days, became one of the most important cities for the Ottoman Empire. After the end of the Russian-Turkish war, Kerch went under the authority of the Russian Empire. Since then, the city has undergone various stages of development, collapsing, rebuilding and again collapsing. Now it is one of the most popular resort towns of the Crimean coast, where you can have a good rest and get acquainted with the culture of locals.

In Kerch, there are a lot of preserved monuments of different epochs. The Yenikale Fortress reminds of the reign of the Ottoman Empire. It was built in the 18th century to protect the strait between the Azov and Black Sea. At the end of the 19th century, the fortress lost its strategic status and was in disrepair. For the years of its existence, the defense constructions have never been reconstructed, so the fortress is partially destroyed now.

Near it, there is the historic monument of the later period, the Kerch Fortress. It was built in the 19th century to protect the borders of the Russian Empire. The fortress is located on Cape Ak-Burun. In the first half of the 20th century, the fortress served as an arsenal. This historical monument had been used for the local military units until 2003. Then, the fortress was declared a tourist attraction. Now, it is located in the open-air museum.

The most remarkable religious monument of Kerch is the Temple of St. John Prodromos. It was built in the 6th century. The church was reconstructed for the first time in the 8th century. Some of its architectural elements are the preserved remains of the first buildings. The temple gained its present design when it was rebuilt in the 10th century. It is still working today. In the temple, you can see interesting old church utensils and the collection of old icons.

In the surroundings of the city, there are several unique archeological districts that are available for tours. Those who are interested in ancient history should see the ruins of the ancient Greek city Panticapaeum. It was formed in the 7th century BC. During its heyday, the city was incredibly wealthy. On its territory, there were luxurious temples and palaces. This big city had existed until the 4th century AD. Now, on the territory of the archeological complex, you can see only some fragments of the magnificent constructions.

In the city, there is the Historical and Archaeological Museum founded in 1926. The museum lost the significant part of its collection during the Crimean War. Today, you can see here archeological artifacts that were found when the city and its surroundings were explored. The museum stores the collections of old weapons, rite tools, accessories, and household items. In total, the museum houses almost 240 000 exhibits, some of which are aged over 2 000 years.

Culture: sights to visit

Culture of Kerch. Places to visit old town, temples, theaters, museums and palaces

Kerch is one of the most ancient cities of Ukraine, and therefore there are many interesting sites that are worth seeing. The city will be interesting especially for those who are fond of history. Considering how many nations lived on these lands, it is not at all surprising that they left behind a rich heritage. Here are the ruins of the ancient Panticapaeum, whose age is more than 2 thousand years.

One of the attractions of Kerch - Kerch fortress, formerly known as Totleben. It was built relatively recently, in the second half of the XIX century; this is a real example of military and engineering art of the time. The fortress was built in the very place where the famous Pavlovsk battery was located before, and even before that the fortresses built by the Turks, Genoese and the ancient Greeks rose proudly. A lot of legends are devoted to this place. It is recommended to inspect the fortress only in the company of a guide, because there are rumors that there are still many military traps in the fortress since the very days when it defended the city and had the most important strategic importance.

Quite famous historical facilities are the Kerch quarries where limestone was actively mined in its time. The sizes of the quarries are amazing the total length of the tunnels is about 40 kilometers. The quarries are divided into three levels, which were laid at different times.

The most curious tourists need to visit the Valley of mud volcanoes, which is only 10 kilometers from the city. The valley looks very picturesque and is located almost next to the Sea of Azov and there are really a lot of small volcanoes here, among them are hydrogen sulphide and even methane. The spectacle is exciting, besides, the size of the valley is not small- several square kilometers.

Kerch museums are also quite interesting; their collections include many unique exhibits. Very interesting is the exposition from the Imperal Mound, excavations of the ancient Greet cities of Ilurat, Tiriaka and Nymphaeus, some excavations from Mount Mithridates and the crypt of the goddess Demeter with truly unique frescoes. In the Historical and Archeological Museum, there is a huge amount of cultural values. There is a collection of ceramics, as well as a lot of objects of Scythian culture and marble statues of past centuries.

Attractions & nightlife
City break in Kerch. Active leisure ideas for Kerch attractions, recreation and nightlife

Kerch provides its guests with all conditions for an interesting and varied stay. In a warm time, the resort town is visited by a huge number of beach lovers. The most lively and popular among holidaymakers is the City Beach, which for several months a year turns into a real entertainment center. Here you can not only sunbathe, but also devote rest to a variety of water activities. On the beach at the height of the season there are several excellent cafes, so you can relax here comfortably for days on end.

In the immediate vicinity of the beach is a beautiful promenade - the most romantic and beautiful place in the city. It is ideal for leisurely walks and intense photo sessions. The Kerch quay is beautiful at any time of the year. In the warm season next to the embankment there is an excellent amusement park, which is worth visiting by all lovers of thrills and holidaymakers with children. It will be pleasant to walk along the embankment and for fans of shopping, as it is the location of a wide variety of souvenir tents.

Kerch does not lack in modern entertainment complexes. At the peak of popularity among holidaymakers remains the center of "Volcano". It can offer its guests a huge selection of slot machines, a bar in the "Wild West" style and a quiet billiard room, and poker tournaments are held several times a week in the center. The entertainment complex "Disney Park" is more suitable for holidaymakers with children, which is part of a large shopping and entertainment center

"Mega". It amazes with an abundance of playgrounds and attractions, among which suitable ones will be found for the youngest and for older children. Every day, the entertainment center hosts colorful performances for visitors. Having tried all the attractions in action, visitors of the shopping and entertainment complex can stroll around the shops or relax in one of the picturesque cafes.

For those who prefer to continue the entertainment program with the arrival of the evening, Kerch has a decent selection of night clubs and bars. The night club Cherry is in demand among guests, and for those who like karaoke, it's worth spending an evening at the club "Kiwi". This is a very cozy and hospitable club, which has an excellent recreation area, and a magnificent bar.

Cuisine & restaurants

Cuisine of Kerch for gourmets. Places for dinner best restaurants
Tatar cuisines are widely represented in Kerch, as the Tatar people have lived on these lands from ancient times. For those who want to get acquainted with the national cuisine, it is worth to go to some nice restaurant and trying branded hot dishes, which locals give a special place on the menu. For first dishes here a wide variety is offered, from the usual vegetable soups, to saturated soups with the addition of dough and groats. The classic first dishes of the Tatar cuisine are vegetable soups, as Crimea since ancient times was rich in plant foods.

Some of the most popular dishes are soups with noodles and other ingredients from dough.

Dumplings for indigenous people, is a special dish, they greet guests. They are served only with broth, and nothing else. In the filling is often added not only meat, but also cottage cheese, and sometimes peas. For the preparation of second courses, meat, potatoes and cereals are increasingly used. Often, the meat that is served on the second course before now was cooked in soup, which is served on the first. Like many centuries ago, meat in national cooking is widespread, but more in boiled or stewed form, than in fried.

"Bales" is one of the oldest dishes of the Tatar cuisine, it is prepared from meat and cereals. Meat should be necessarily fatty, most often for cooking dishes pork is used, and from cereals barley or millet is preferred. Another dish of Tatar cuisine, which now may seem quite exotic, is a finely chopped liver with rice, which is placed in a natural shell and baked. This classic Tatar dish is called "tutyrma".

There are a lot of dairy dishes in the Tatar cuisine, however, dough occupies the main place and the Tatars treat it with special respect. The most popular type of baked goods which must be tried is pies with pumpkin filling, in which sometimes millet or rice is added. The filling with pumpkin patty is the most popular, but Tatars bake pies and stuff them with beets and carrots, this combination may seem quite unusual to many. Tea has long become a traditional Tatar drink, without which no dinner or party is held. Tea is drunk by everyone, they are drunk in different versions, and tea simply requires sweets, especially sweets from dough with the addition of honey and nuts.

Kharkov

Guide to Kharkov

Sightseeing in Kharkov what to see. Complete travel guide
The city was founded in the beginning of the 17th century. At that time here was built a powerful fortress aimed at protecting Russian land from the raids of the Tatars. Starting from the late 18th century Kharkov has been known as a major shopping district, a university center and a city with great cultural and historical heritage. Nowadays you can learn more about the history and the glorious past of this city in numerous museums, monuments and buildings.

Start the exploration of the city from its main street Sumskaya Street. Here you will see beautiful houses built in the 18th - 19th centuries. The street is stretched between two large squares. Constitution Square is the location of Historical Museum that exhibits all important and valuable pre-revolution artifacts. Opposite to the museum you will see Shevchenko Theatre. The theater is surrounded by Poetry Park - one of the most romantic places in the city. Dzerzhinsky Square is present in the list of the three largest squares in the world. Despite its huge size the square is always quiet and cozy. This is a great place to forget about stressful and noisy city life. The square has become a popular music concerts venue. Here are often conducted numerous festivals, and weekends is the time for fairs, on which you can buy numerous interesting accessories and handicrafts.

Not far from Sumskaya Street is located another sight, the botanical garden, which is a truly beautiful corner of wilderness formed around a pure stream. The choice of plants and flowers here is simply amazing; many species have been imported from exotic countries and have adapted wonderfully to the local climate. The botanic garden is also the start of a ropeway. Use the funicular to get to another beautiful place Gorky Park. This is the best place for families with children, as you will find here several entertainment centers. Guests are welcome to play paintball, ride on the miniature railway or have a picnic.

In Kharkiv, there are a lot of beautiful religious monuments. One of the most impressive is St. Peter and St. Paul Church. It was built in 1866. Today, many tourists easily recognize this church due to its pinnacle and black dome. The old church is one of the few temples in the city that was not almost damaged during the Second World War. It was constantly open even in wartime. In 1996, the church was completely reconstructed and then served as a church school.

The religious monument of the later period is the Annunciation Cathedral built at the beginning of the 20th century. Despite the fact that the age of the cathedral is only a hundred years, it is a luxurious example of the Byzantium style. The building is distinguished by a fascinating design of its dome, facade and interior.

In Kharkiv, there is a unique art museum. Its collection was started over 200 years ago, in 1805. Over the years of its existence, the museum collection has been expanded significantly. This building has been housing the collection since 1912. It is presented in 25 halls and divided on the basis of time periods. The visitors of the museum have an opportunity to see unique masterpieces of European and Russian artists. The age of some paintings is over 300 years.

When walking along Kharkiv, you can admire a lot of beautiful fountains. One of the most unusual fountains is the Mirror Stream. It was constructed in 1947 after the victory in the Second World War. This fascinating fountain is a complex of the fountain itself and the beautiful pavilion. In 2007, it was completely reconstructed and now is furnished with beautiful marble. In the evening, it is illuminated with over 130 spotlights.

When walking along Sumska Street, you should definitely drop in the shopping mall called Platinum Plaza. There is the original Garden of Sculptures where you can take a lot of spectacular pictures. The initiator of its opening is collector Alexander Feldman. He presented several sculptures from his private collection for decorating the patio. Today, you can see even masterpieces of famous Israeli sculptor Frank Meisler here.

Culture: sights to visit

Culture of Kharkov. Places to visit old town, temples, theaters, museums and palaces

Kharkov is ready to offer its guests a huge number of exciting excursions. Ancient streets and squares, famous historical sites and monuments, churches, museums, theaters and landscaped gardens are among its attractions. The largest square of the country is situated in Kharkov; we are talking about Freedom Square. The scenic square was founded in the first half of the 20th century; it is the main venue for national celebrations and cultural events. The square is also popular among hikers.

Kharkov was severely damaged during World War II, but a significant portion of its architectural monuments remained intact. The beautiful monument, the Mirror Stream fountain designed in the Empire style, reminds people about victory of Soviets. Its grand opening was held in 1947.

The Governor's Palace is considered to be the most outstanding architectural monument of the 18th century. Construction of the palace was completed in 1777; it is notable because of harmonious combination of different architectural styles. Currently, the part of the beautiful Palace is housing Ukrainian Engineering and Pedagogical Academy.

The most famous monument in the Art Nouveau style is the House with Chimeras; the facade of the building is decorated with interesting sculptural elements. In addition to chimeras, you can see the old knight's coat of arms, as well as salamanders and wolves. Kharkov is famous for its outstanding religious and tourist attractions, the most famous of which is the Cathedral of the Annunciation.

The first church on the site of the cathedral had been founded back in 1655; it has been repeatedly destroyed and rebuilt completely. The Cathedral has gained its name only in the mid-19th century. Several priceless religious relics are stored there. Among other religious objects Basil's Cathedral and Cathedral of the Assumption should be mentioned; the latter has being unchanged from the mid-19th century. The city has dozens of interesting museums and excellent theaters. The Historical Museum, the Art Museum, the Museum of Popular Arts and the Maritime Museum have to be included in the must-see program. Fans of theater arts will be delighted by the Lysenko Theater of Opera and Ballet; younger visitors will love the Puppet Theatre.

Attractions & nightlife

City break in Kharkov. Active leisure ideas for Kharkov attractions, recreation and nightlife
Kharkov offers a large selection of beautiful parks. The Gorky Park and Shevchenko Park are considered to be the most fascinating ones, and

in the warmer months, a family just won't find a better place to stay. Shevchenko Park is famous for the exquisite design; its territory houses the Kharkov Dolphinarium. There is also an unusual monument to a soccer ball; every day it attracts sports fans making photos with it. Gorky Park has plenty of diverse rides; there is a great Ferry wheel and play areas for young children in it.

Those preferring to spend time outdoors would be in visiting the Kharkov Zoo, which is home to exotic animals. There are tigers and leopards, bears and mountain sheep, falcons and peacocks among its inhabitants. Visitors are allowed to feed animals and take pictures with them.

Atmosphere mall invites visitors to play bowling and spend time in a comfortable ambience. In addition to the bowling center, its territory has several attractive cafes and bars; close to the entertainment complex there are popular restaurants and modern cinemas.

Fans of night entertainment like the Misto club; it has attractive decor and an abundance of branded treats. Visitors will appreciate the carefully planned entertainment program at Misto. The original Arizona beach club is especially in demand among tourists in warmer months. The leisure facilities at the club are fitted around the small pool making the stay even more enjoyable.

Fans of shopping won't be bored too, as there are countless shops and ultramodern shopping complexes in Kharkov. Among them, Sun City, Prism and Cascade shopping complexes are worth mentioning. The Ukraine shopping and entertainment complex is ready to offer its visitors an abundance of interesting and original products and leisure options. If you look for souvenirs and fashion accessories, you can go to the Imperia shopping mall; there you could find goods for every taste and budget.

Cuisine & restaurants

Cuisine of Kharkov for gourmets. Places for dinner best restaurants
Holidays in Kharkov would be incomplete without a visit to local restaurants; some of them are very unusual and attractive places. One of the best restaurants in the city is Vzletayushiy Drakon; it specializes in Asian cuisine. The restaurant's menu is dominated by popular Chinese, Vietnamese and Japanese dishes, but there is a number of treats for fans of European cuisine. The restaurant has a beautiful banquet hall, so it is perfect for large-scale events.

The Victoria restaurant offers its guests top Ukrainian dishes. The place has a very impressive decor. The restaurant serves visitors almost around the clock, so you can have a family breakfast or a romantic dinner there.

Those preferring exotic signature dishes are recommended to visit the Alibi restaurant. The menu there provides a decent selection of fish and meat dishes. Regulars especially appreciate bay scallops with mango sauce and stuffed quail. Fans of meats are recommended to taste ostrich fillet cooked on the grill with a side dish of caramelized apples.

The Araks restaurant invites visitors to relax in the unique medieval ambience and enjoy signature treats. This is a professional restaurant that specializes in gourmet dishes; it is ideal for banquets. Visitors can get acquainted with Caucasian cuisine. Guests can relax in the cozy bar or in the billiard room.

The gastronomic complex Zolotoy Grill would be a perfect holiday destination, which in addition to an abundance of attractive restaurants, cafes and bars, offers a wide range of entertainment. There is a cozy pub and a beautiful outdoor cafe, upscale wine bar, first-class restaurant for kids, stylish sports bar and barbecue there. Decor of gastronomic complex is made in a unique Greek style. Fans of Chinese cuisine are advised to visit the China Town restaurant located in the heart of the city, on the territory of one of the famous hotels. A selection of treats here is just huge. Chefs can also cook delicious Chinese food on demand.

Traditions & lifestyle
Colors of Kharkov traditions, festivals, mentality and lifestyle
Kharkov has a special charm due to its unique cultural atmosphere. It is the city with beautiful centuries-old traditions and rich cultural life.

Local residents are cheerful and optimistic; they like to have fun and know how to do that. That's why an abundance of fun-filled holidays is held there. Locals also feature a wonderful sense of humor; fans of excursions and walks will notice this feature of the national character.

The fact is that the city has an incredible amount of interesting monuments along with an abundance of religious and historical sites. Lots of beautiful monuments are dedicated to outstanding literary characters; there is also a monument of the soccer ball, as well as colorful and highly original frog monument in the city. The search of original monuments remains one of the most popular entertainment options, as they can be found literally on every street of Kharkov.

Event tourists are encouraged to visit the city on the eve of New Year holidays. During this period, the city transforms beyond recognition. The familiar and beloved festival is celebrated here in a special manner; the magical transformation of Kharkov begins long before the actual onset of the New Year. Every day, city streets are becoming more festive and colorful; they are decorated with authentic Christmas items and festive illumination.

The main Christmas tree of the city is set on Freedom Square; it strikes with its size. Each year ornaments for the Christmas tree are made by expert craftsmen. During the New Year holiday, Freedom square is the most fun and lively place. A wide variety of rides is set there for children. Numerous stalls and kiosks wait for fans of sweets and traditional treats.

The integral part of the Christmas holidays in Kharkov is represented by colorful fairs. At 24th of December of each year Freedom Square hosts a large international fair, where residents of foreign countries represent their products. Fairs are held in full compliance with national traditions; instead of usual stalls vacationers can see colorful dolly-shops. Residents of sister cities of Kharkov take active part in organization of Christmas events; this period is considered one of the most soulful and attractive.

Tips for tourists

Preparing your trip to Kharkov: advices & hints things to do and to obey

1. Trams and trolleybuses are considered main means of public transport; they move freely throughout the territory of Kharkov. Tickets are purchased from a busman or a driver. The city also has a rather unusual form of transport, the cable way.

2. Banks and other government agencies serve visitors from 9:00 am to 5:00 pm; some large institutions can work up to 7:00 pm. Foreigners can exchange currency not only in banks, but also in specialized exchange offices with quite ample working hours.

3. In restaurants and cafes you can leave a tip for good service; the sum making out 5 - 10% of the total would be appropriate. The service charge in upscale restaurants is often included in the total; it is rarely more than 10% of the total bill.

4. Tourists are advised to book tickets for sightseeing tours and cultural events in advance. You can order them at any tour desk or directly at the hotel; this way you would avoid long queues and could plan your vacation in advance.

5. To rent a car you have to have a passport and a driving license issued at least two years ago. The cost of car rent depends on the selected brand and starts from 30 USD daily. Those under 21 years old may be denied service.

6. Tourists who come to Kharkov as a big company are recommended to use taxi. Note that there are two types of tariffs, day and night; the last is about half as much again the daily one.

7. Indigenous people are very welcoming and hospitable, so travelers from different countries would feel comfortable in Kharkov. It's worth to learn a few simple phrases in the Ukrainian to pay respect for locals; this act is sure to be appreciated.

8. There are excellent facilities for a family holiday in Kharkov; a number of local entertainment places offer reasonable discounts to

visitors with children. It is profitable to have some tours as a company, because in this case you can save considerably.

Kherson

Guide to Kherson
Sightseeing in Kherson what to see. Complete travel guide
Kherson is famous as a big industrial center and a river port. For many travelers, the city is a starting point to explore the outstanding attractions of Central Ukraine. Kherson is interesting as a separate tourist center too. In the territory of the city, there are many important historical objects. Pleasant recreation in Kherson is guaranteed not only to those who prefer walking along historical places, but also to those who can't imagine their vacation without visiting gastronomic places. Tourists are attracted by many restaurants. There are modest budget places, as well as prestigious venues for wealthy visitors.

One of the main distinctive features of modern Kherson is an opportunity to organize a vacation of any level. It will delight those travelers who have got used to luxury and high-level service, as well as those who don't spend too much money during their vacation. The entertainment industry in Kherson deserves the highest praise. The city is famous for its upscale sports centers, colorful disco and nightclubs, family entertainment centers and cinemas. You can travel to Kherson in any season. Due to its close proximity to the Black Sea

Coast, more tourists visit it in summer. In the warm season, the main travelers' entertainment is beach recreation and walking along picturesque places. Those who don't like beaches prefer visiting Kherson in the off-season or in winter. It should be noted that the prices for hotel accommodation are very attractive at this time. So, even a big company can vacation here for a reasonable price.

In Kherson, there is an excellent tourist center that is located in the building of the Fregat Hotel and is open all year round. No matter what the season is, travelers can take many interesting excursion and entertainment programs. Certainly, the city won't disappoint fans of excursions. Enchanting squares and the mysterious Old Town shrouded in interesting legends, picturesque streets with lots of green plantings and spectacular architectural constructions, the romantic embankment and plenty of symbolic monuments reminding of the most important events in the city history... This is how Kherson appears to its guests.

In the surroundings of Kherson, there are a lot of nature attractions. One of them is the unique biosphere nature park Askania Nova. It was founded by one of the local dukes at the beginning of the 19th century. Originally, rich natural grounds were used to herd ships. Today, you can see here rare plants and admire birds and rare insects. The nature park is very big. There are a lot of different hiking routes. In 1973, the nature park gained a status of the attraction of state significance. It is interesting to admire its wonderful landscapes at any time of the year.

The important historic attraction is Kherson Church. It started to be built in the second half of the 18th century. The defensive construction had been used as intended until 1866. When the fortress lost its strategic status, it came to the city government. In the second half of the 19th century, many constructions in the territory of the fortress were destroyed. New houses were built of stone in the city center. Today, the visitors of the fortress can see the preserved arsenal, several old wells, bastions, and tinderboxes руку.

The interesting religious monument is the Cathedral of St. Katherine. It became the first stone cathedral built in the city territory. It was being built at the same time as the Kherson Fortress. Now, the cathedral is a vivid example of Russian classicism. After the Revolution, the cathedral was closed and all the values were transferred. Originally, it served as an anti-religious museum and then as a warehouse. The cathedral was reopened in 1991. Despite its complicated history, it has preserved many original interior elements.

One of the most luxurious buildings of Kherson is occupied by the art museum called after A. Shovkunenko. The luxurious building with its fascinating facade was built in 1906 and belonged to the City Duma from the beginning. The museum collection started to be formed in 1890. Initially, its collection was quite modest. Nowadays, the museum houses over 7 000 exhibits, including unique paintings of the 17th century. The historic building is distinguished by a luxurious design and has a great architectural value.

Kiev

Guide to Kiev

Sightseeing in Kiev what to see. Complete travel guide
In order to get acquainted with all notable places of Kiev you will need more than one day of long walks. However, you will not need any transport as all main sights of this city are located nearby.

The main street of the city is called Kreschatik. We suggest starting your observation of the city with it. It's also worth mentioning that this street is one of the widest in the world. On weekends the movement of the transport is closed on Kreschatik, so pedestrians can enjoy various architectural sights of this place, look at monuments and sculptures. The buildings on the street were made in different epochs, so their combination is unusual and very interesting to visitors. Here you will find numerous modern restaurants that offer wide selection of national and European dishes, and multiple trading centers and boutiques.

Theatre connoisseurs should make a walk on Gorodetsky Street and look at Ivan Franko Theater. President Palace is located nearby. There you can also see one more interesting building the House with Chimeras.

One more interesting place, Golden Gates, is located not far away from the main street. Once these ancient gates have been the main entrance of the city. When guests entered Kiev, the first thing they saw St. Sophia Cathedral built in the 11th century. Today its walls keep a large collection of relics and frescos that traditionally amaze people. The opposite side of the St. Sophia Square is the place of the location of Bogdan Khmelnitsky monument and St. Michael's Cathedral. When you are tired from walks in this city, you can make a funicular ride that features a magnificent view of Kiev. These are just some memorable places that are worth visiting when you are in Kiev.

In Kiev, there is a unique ancient monastery the Kiev-Pechersk Lavra. It was founded in the 11th century and is now a UNESCO site. The monastery is a compound architectural center with several temples, a theological seminary and other buildings. Even the oldest part was retained - the cells that were carved directly into the rock. In addition to religious relics, the monastery houses a rich collection of books. One of the largest state libraries in the country is located here.

Among the religious attractions, the Saint Sophia's Cathedral, deserves special attention. The first mention of it dates back to the 13th century. For hundreds of years of its existence, the cathedral has been repeatedly destroyed, but was quickly restored and each time it became bigger and more spectacular. Now the cathedral is also considered a site of world heritage. The last major reconstruction in it was held in the 17th century. In the cathedral, many old decoration elements have been preserved. At present, services are held exclusively on major religious holidays.

The beautiful Saint Andrew's Church is considered one of the most spectacular in the world of monuments in the Baroque style. This church was built in the middle of the 18th century. It is located in the heart of the historical district of Kiev, on top of a hill. The temple impresses with its beauty. Its domes are painted in emerald color, and the facade is executed in a white-blue style. In this church, precious elements of decoration were also preserved. Many ancient icons and other shrines are kept in it.

In Kiev, there are many outstanding architectural monuments. A spectacular example of the Art Nouveau style is the House with Chimaeras. The main feature of this original mansion is the sculptures decorating its facade, on which mythical creatures - chimeras are depicted. The interior of this mansion is no less original. The author of the building project was the famous architect Wladyslaw Horodecki.

The National Museum of History of Ukraine remains the most visited cultural institution in Kiev. Once it was founded like a small archeological exhibition. With time, the museum's exposition grew thousands of times. The official opening of the museum took place in

1904. Presently, in addition to unique archeological artifacts, one can see extensive collections of weapons, ancient coins, rare books, porcelain, and art products.

Top sightseeing

Top architectural sightseeing and landmarks of Kiev ideas on city exploration routes

Kiev Pechersk Lavra, St. Andrew Church, Monument of Independence, and St. Michael Golden-Domed Monastery are the architectural landmarks for not only tourists, but also for residents of Kiev. The majority of these monuments were created several centuries ago. They witnessed many important events, so besides the architectural value for Ukraine, these landmarks are of a great historic importance. In this review, you will be able to get acquainted with the main architectural sites of Kiev. Also, we will look at them from an unusual point of view only interesting facts and photos, which come together with a 3D visualization of every monument. Use our unique technology to fly over all architectural places of interest of Kiev the video is at your fingertips.

Kiev Pechersk Lavra, Kiev

Facts: » In the 11th century, a priest dug a hole in the ground in a forest to serve the Lord in seclusion. The followers joined him. Constructions began to arise.

» Nowadays, the Kiev Pechersk Lavra (it means "street") is a monastery complex with 14 Orthodox monasteries. There are museums, a functioning monastery, a printing house, bell towers 41 buildings in total. The area occupied is 30 hectares.

» The objects that are particularly revered are the remains of the departed men of God who did a lot for the country. Wonder-working icons are brought here.

» The holy site is located on two elevations by the Dnieper River. The white-stone Dormition Church (1073) is considered to be the main temple.

» The landmark of the place is underground passages stretching for 400 meters. The grottoes are 15 meters deep. They have churches and crypts.

» The relics are put in wooden boxes and covered with mantels. Some have wrists that are able to be seen to show that a body is not destroyed by decomposition.

» Three myrrh-leaking heads rest in cells. Studies showed that the fragrant organic oil has healing properties. The phenomenon defies scientific laws.

St. Andrew Church, Kiev

Facts: » The stone Orthodox church was laid on the site of a former fortress bastion on top of a mountain in 1744.

» The builders had to construct a 15-meter-high ground part under the base of the building to make it stronger and prevent it from being destroyed by groundwater.

» It had been intended to be built by the time Empress Elizabeth I came to the area as part of her pilgrimage to Kiev.

» The shape of the 47-meter house resembles an elongated cross. The church is covered with a huge dark green dome. It is decorated with gilded garlands. There are turrets rising on four sides.

» Stucco molding and cast iron were used to decorate the walls of a religious building for the first time.

» Turquoise walls contrast with snow-white colonnades and decorations in the form of unfolded scrolls. All items are gilded.

» The interior is as picturesque as the exterior. All frescoes picture biblical themes. Their distinctive feature is thoroughly painted details in the characters' costumes, their poses, still lifes, nature pictures. Such painting is not typical of cult asceticism.

» 39 icons for a 3-tier carved iconostasis had been created by a Ukrainian artist for 3 years.

» The church is named for Andrew the Apostle.

Monument of Independence , Kiev

Facts: » The 42-meter triumphal column is located on the square in the center of the city. An architect from Kiev worked on its construction.

» The vertical structure is faced with light Italian marble brought from the Mediterranean.

» To make it more stable, a reinforced concrete frame was installed inside the stela. A 1.5-ton counterweight was also placed there so that the monument could resist the forces of nature. It can hold back the flow of a hurricane wind and ground movements. There are spiral stairs leading to the top.

» The elevation resembles a temple.

» A statue of a girl in a long shirt rises in the middle of the monument. It is a symbol personifying the Mother of God with open arms. Her all-embracing gesture means intercessory prayer. The guelder rose branch in the hands, embroidery on the dress, and headdress ribbons are painted in gold leaf. Guelder rose has always been considered a symbol of Ukraine.

» The statue of Berehynia itself is cast in bronze. It weighs about 20 tons. The sculptor's daughter served as a model for the female figure.

» Three projects were selected by the jury of the competition. They formed the basis of the design.

» The monument commemorates the independence of the state and was built on the occasion of its 10th anniversary.

St. Michael Golden-Domed Monastery, Kiev

Facts: » The church complex consists of a cathedral, refectory, church, and a bell tower.

» According to legend, the monastery was founded by the first bishop of the city. The temple dedicated to the archangel was ordered by the grandson of Yaroslav the Wise (1113) as the evangelist was the heavenly patron of the townspeople.

» The facade cladding mixes flat brick masonry and rows of stone.

» It was the first time in the history of architecture when a dome was gilded on a religious building, which is why it is called 'Golden-Domed'.

» Princes of Kiev rest in this place.

» The interior of the hall is lined with mosaic panels. There were times when such images stretched along all the walls.

» Only 45 square meters of the original several-century-old mosaics remained intact. The pictures are called flickering as the patterns were selected in such a way that it seems the shades are opalescent.

» The community was presented with a gift from Emperor Alexander I. He gave the icon of St. Michael into their possession. The frame is made of pure gold and decorated with diamond inserts.

» There is an altar canopy in the monastery courtyard. It has a stone fountain bowl from where a spring comes out. It is furnished with picturesque columns and adorned with frescoes. The bowl is covered with a gilded coating.

Kiev Fortress, Kiev

Facts: » The fortifications of the ancient fortress form a whole complex. The constructions of the kind had been built since the 12th century. Fortified wall panels were erected specially for reinforcement.

» Emperor of All Russia Peter I personally ordered the construction of the powerful citadel.

» The defensive complex was completed in 1723.

» The fortress had through passages built in the second half of the 18th century.

» Museum exhibits tell visitors about the history of the rampart called the Kosyi Caponier ("Skew Caponier").

» Initially, three rope roads led to the fortification. The cableway was used to deliver building materials, ammunition, and soldiers.

» Special hollows that could immediately fill with water were dug. There was enough power to overturn enemy ships. There's evidence of the facts in the chronicles.

» The museum complex exhibits the relics of the former construction: personal award badges, soldiers' uniforms, weapon arsenal.

» The wagon that transported prisoners sentenced to death from cells to the military fort remained intact. The last prisoner in the punishment cell was the designer of the fortress.

Church of the Saviour at Berestove, Kiev

Facts: » In the heyday of Kievan Rus, there was a village where the Kiev nobility used to stay. The settlement was surrounded by a birch forest. Hence the name the village of Berestovo ('береста' (beresta) means 'birch bark').

» The villagers had their own church. It's mentioned in the chronicles of 1051.

» In 1157, Yuri Dolgorukiy, the founder of Moscow, found the last shelter here. A sarcophagus-like tombstone was put on the place where the prince was buried.

» Many centuries later, a bell tower was built near the main building.

» The original brickwork the stripes of pink mortar and slabs was partially preserved in the church.

» The interior has a 12th-century fresco called Miraculous Fishing. The painting pictures the apostles catching fish from a lake.

» The walls were painted by the masters invited from Athos.

» Today, the house of God looks like a five-headed building. The last renovation transformed the Church of the Savior at Berestovo. The roofing was repaired, and the domes were gilded. The temple that went through many alterations during the history is still functioning.

» In 1900, during archaeological excavations, the slate tombs, presumably from the time of Ancient Rus, were found here.

Mother Motherland, Kiev

Facts: » The unbreakable spirit of the nation that managed to go through the terrible patriotic war is embodied in the 102-meter monument standing on the city's highest point. It can be seen from afar.

» A female figure with a shield and a sword reflects the image of a protector.

» Sculptors, construction engineers, surveyors, and scientists worked on the commemorative monument.

» A slope was drilled 34 meters deep to fix and construct a 32-meter-high base. The metal frame and skin were cast in Zaporozhye, after which experts welded solid stainless steel sheets on site.

» The entire structure weighs 450 tons, the sword is 9 tons, the shield with an emblem is 13 tons.

» It's still a mystery what happened with the tower crane used to build the monument. Some say it was dismantled and dumped into the Dnieper.

» The monument can withstand the ground movement of magnitude 8.0. There's a device at the top of it that controls wind gusts.

» The hollow inside of the statue allows using two lifts to reach the observation platform in 12 minutes. The cab can hold two people. There are stairs installed in narrow parts of the figure.

» A sculpture of this size had not been made in the USSR before.

Family trip with kids

Family trip to Kiev with children. Ideas on where to go with your child

The selection of entertainment for holidaymakers with children in Kiev is simply wide. They should definitely visit the Kiev Zoo. In this large zoo, you can see animals from all over the world. In the zoo, giraffes, elephants, tigers and monkeys, live in spacious enclosures and there is also a very remarkable terrarium with snakes, lizards and turtles. The territory of the zoo is equipped with a large number of playgrounds for children, and a variety of attractions are installed. There are also cozy cafes in operation here. In this amazing picturesque place, you can comfortably relax all day long.

A no less attractive place is the Oceanarium "Sea Fairy Tale" - a large and beautifully equipped aquarium with a rich collection of inhabitants of the underwater world. Visitors of the center will have the opportunity to observe rare tropical fish and dangerous marine predators that swim in large aquariums, and they will also be able to walk along a transparent tunnel and observe the sharks that float above their heads. The oceanarium is distinguished by a spectacular design, and all its halls are lit up by artistic illumination. After viewing the collection, visitors can look into the gift shop and purchase mesmerizing gifts of marine themes.

The dolphinarium "Nemo" is very popular among holidaymakers with children in Kiev. It is indoors, therefore accessible for visiting all year round. Effective performances with the participation of trained dolphins are conducted in it daily. For an additional fee, visitors to the center can swim in one pool with the most amazing inhabitants of the aquatic depths, and also make an excellent commemorative photo session.

A few years ago, was the opening of the original zoo "Ecoland" in Kiev, which today is equally loved by tourists and locals. Among the inhabitants of this indoor zoo are colorful parrots, iguanas, snakes, hedgehogs, lemurs, and other representatives of the tropical forests. Visitors can hold in their hands and feed all the animals in this zoo. Also, visitors are invited to make excellent photos for memory. In the zoo, very remarkable cognitive excursions are held for children.

There are dozens of entertainment centers in Kiev. One of the most popular is KidsWill. It is aimed at young children. In this center, kids are offered the opportunity to get acquainted with the peculiarities of various professions. They can learn in a game form what the work of doctors and sellers are, and also how a fire truck is arranged and how it works. Remarkable entertaining activities and lessons on creativity are regularly conducted in the center for children.

The entertainment center "Igroland" is also suitable for young children. It is indoors, and is distinguished by an impressive scale. The entertainment complex is brightly decorated, and has playrooms for both the youngest and the school-age children. Slot machines, dry pools, a variety of attractions, a great café - all that you need for a fun-filled holiday with children can be seen here.

An ideal museum to visit with children will be Experimentarium. This is a modern museum dedicated to science and technology. Literally all of its exhibits are interactive; you can touch them with your hands. An excursion around the museum is always accompanied by mesmerizing experiments, so it is sure to please children hungry for new knowledge and impressions. The museum regularly holds fascinating themed events, including unusual acoustic shows.

Unusual weekend

How to spend top weekend in Kiev ideas on extraordinary attractions and sites

Already had a chance to explore spectacular architectural sights of Kiev and wonder about diversifying leisure with something else? It's time to go underground and see the unique underground rivers, which are one of the little-known attractions of the city. The most famous among them is the River Khreshchatyk, which flows under the central street of the same name. The River Clove originates close to Arsenalna metro station. In total, Kyiv has several dozen underground rivers. Some collectors were built in the late 19th century. Of course, there are no organized tours here; however, experienced guides from among locals are always happy to come to the aid of curious tourists.

Another great way to enjoy the beauty of dungeons is to take the Kiev Metro. Some stations are striking with their rich decoration, and Metro Golden Gate Station is among the most spectacular ones. Gorgeous natural stone elements, huge medieval-style chandeliers, and painted vaulted ceilings - a visit to this place is akin to exploring a medieval castle.

Like to play computer games preferring the most difficult quests? If yes, go to an original game room at 9 Borysoglebska Street. At this address, Claustrophobia Escape Room (Real Quest Claustrophobia) invites its guests to go through an exciting quest based on books about Sherlock Holmes in real life. Reliably hidden caches, difficult puzzles and keys - the quest will fascinate even to those who've never been interested in computer games.

Fans of conceptual art will not be bored in Kyiv too - they'll have a chance to stroll through the original Fashion Park. It is located on the Landscape Alley, being a collection of original art installations. One of the park's main features is unusual benches sitting on which you can take a lot of great photos.

After walking in unusual places, it's time to go shopping and look for original gifts for loved ones. For unique handmade souvenirs, go to "Pravda, b" Shop (However, b) sharing one building with the One Street Museum located on Andriyivskyy Descent. Here you can buy a lot of original hand-painted statuettes, interesting paintings, and knitwear, as well as a lot of interesting national-style handicrafts.

For fashionable clothes, go to Puree Shop at 21 Reitarska Street. One of the most modern and trendy shops in Kyiv surprises customers not only with the variety of stylish clothes for every taste but also with its original urban-style design.

Kyiv has a lot of attractive museums and art galleries. One of the most original cultural institutions is Bauhaus Center. Located on

Dehtiarivska Street, it is a permanent venue for interesting film screenings, hand-made fairs, art and photo exhibitions, as well as other interesting events participated by young talents.

In "Tower No. 5" Business Center, you can visit another original cultural institution - the << Museum of Toilets>>. As you might guess from the name, it is fully devoted to the "toilet" theme. Among the museum's exhibits are unique painted toilet bowls, as well as a lot of interesting photographs depicting priceless historical artifacts. Museum visitors will have a chance to see what the toilet looked like in the prehistoric era and find out what kind of sewage systems medieval castles had.

Culture: sights to visit

Culture of Kiev. Places to visit old town, temples, theaters, museums and palaces

Among the spectacular sights of Kiev there are religious sites, unique monuments of architecture, and a variety of museums, so every traveler could choose an interesting cultural program. Church of St. Andrew is a true sample of the baroque; it was constructed in the second half of the 18th century. The church is located on a high hill. Today this famous religious monument is converted into a museum.

Another interesting historical site is the Kiev Pechersk Lavra. This monastery was founded in 1051; it is one of the oldest monasteries in the world. Kiev Pechersk Lavra is a world-class attraction; in the territory there is the tomb of Peter Stolypin and a lot of religious artifacts.

One of the most unusual and famous monuments is the House with Chimeras. Its construction began in 1901 and lasted for just over a year. The author of the Art Nouveau original is Vladislav Gorodetsky. Another world-class monument is Sophia Cathedral built in the 11th century. Few centuries after the discovery the cathedral was rebuilt; today visitors can see a building in the Baroque style, which has been existing since the 13th century. The cathedral preserved frescoes and mosaics that attract numerous visitors.

St. Vladimir's Cathedral, opened in the late 19th century, is also an important religious site. The work under its construction lasted for almost 50 years. Cathedral features a refined decoration; its walls keep many important religious artifacts. Among the cultural places of the city we should mention Museum of Folk Architecture and Life of Ukraine. This is a large-scale open air museum complex with an exhibition that features more than 300 exhibits. There visitors can see ancient windmills, crafts and household items of indigenous people.

An unusual sight is the Pharmacy Museum, which first welcomed its visitors in 1986. Its collection includes a variety of exhibits related to the pharmacy business, from pharmaceutical instruments and bottles to crabs and snakes preserved in alcohol. The most famous monument of defensive architecture is the Golden Gate, which had served as the main entrance to the city until the 17th century. The powerful fortress tower with a wide thoroughfare has preserved perfectly. Near the gate there is a small museum dedicated to the history of the edifice.

The Kyiv National Academic Theater of Operetta is definitely worth visiting, and not only for its wonderful theater performances. The interior and exterior are striking with their splendor so much that it seems as if this is not a theater building but a royal palace where nobles once lived. However, this does not negate the fact that once tsars indeed attended performances to enjoy the architecture, the interior, and the show. It is worth noting that the theater is a historical site - the 3rd Prime Minister of Russia Pyotr Stolypin who attended "The Tale of Tsar Saltan" together with Tsar Nicholas II and his family was once hilled here. Another cultural institution attractive with its rich interior is the National Organ and Chamber Music Hall of Ukraine that occupies the Roman Catholic Church of St. Nicholas. The construction of this masterpiece of neo-Gothic architecture was completed in 1909.

The National Bank of Ukraine building is a great example of Empire architecture. It was built in1839, and its main pride is griffons installed on the corners of the building. Sightseeing in Kyiv cannot be imagined without exploring Syrotkyna Apartment House - one of the most beautiful buildings in the Ukrainian capital. Facades with baroque, Art Nouveau and neo-renaissance elements, windows in the style of early

Art Nouveau, relief details and sculptures - all this boggles the imagination and makes the heart of every visitor to Kyiv beat faster. A masterpiece of Stalinist Empire style is the Expocenter of Ukraine National Complex where interesting exhibitions are often held. It is also worth noting that this complex was once visited by famous figures such as Margaret Thatcher, Charles de Gaulle, Broz Tito.

A wonderful architectural landmark is the Castle of Richard the Lionheart, so named for its resemblance to castles built during the reign of the king famous for his bravery. All its towers and spires make the castle look like a British Gothic building. By the way, some famous Ukrainian artists lived here at different times. Quite unusual for Kyiv is a French-style quarter with a miniature replica of the Eiffel Tower in its center. Well, those who wish to see not France but Japan would be happy to visit Kyoto Park with its wonderful peaceful atmosphere.

Yagimovskiy House that is often referred to as "House With Cats" is another brilliant architectural creation. It is called so because its main pride is magnificent cat-shaped bas-reliefs. However, the palace had another name - once it was called the "House of Koschei" since the architect's last name was Bezsmertnyi (translates as "Immortal", just like Koschei in Slavic folklore). The building with Art Nouveau elements was completed in 1909 and immediately began to attract the attention of those looking for aesthetic pleasure. Another interesting building in Kyiv is the so-called "Chocolate House", which got its name for a facade resembling the chocolate texture. Built in an eclectic style in1901, the mansion draws the attention of all connoisseurs of architectural art.

The famous Mariyinsky Palace, the pearl of the eponymous park, is no less remarkable for its architectural composition. The palace was built by order of Elizaveta Petrovna, the architects were Bartolomeo Rastrelli, Ivan Michurin and Vasily Neyolov who chose Baroque as the dominant architectural style of the building. The palace was often visited by members of the royal family - for example, by Catherine II and Maria Feodorovna. Later the building served as a revolutionary committee headquarters, a museum, and an agricultural school. Nearby is the Verkhovna Rada of Ukraine building designed by Volodymyr Zabolotny and completed in 1939. Classicism was chosen as the main style. It must be said that the building is attractive for its accuracy and precision - that's how any government building should look like.

Equally interesting are sculptures located throughout the city. These are monuments to great people - Bogdan Khmelnitsky, Taras Shevchenko, Volodymyr the Great, Princess Olga, as well as memorials in honor of Afghan soldiers and people affected by the Chernobyl nuclear disaster. The Motherland Monument, which is a permanent symbol of the unity of Ukraine and its capital's hallmark, is worthy of at least a cursory inspection. Beautiful parks are ideal for walking in

Kyiv. This can be the already mentioned Mariyinsky Park, Shevchenko Park or Natalka Park.

Kyiv is famous for its unique museums. Besides such an original cultural institution as the Toilet History Museum (by the way, it is among the most interesting museums in the world), here you can find the Museum of Dreams with its impressive works of art that arose as if from the subconscious, as well as Mykola Syadristy Microminiatures Museum with its superbly executed and detailed works. It is quite possible to see all Kyiv's attractions in one place - the Ukrainian capital has a unique museum called "Kyiv in miniature" (situated in Hydropark, another great place to walk). Amazing sights created with attention to the smallest details - not only tourists but also locals love this place.

Get acquainted with the traditional way of life of local residents' ancestors in two museums: the first is the Museum of Folk Architecture and Life (Pirogovo) and the second is "Mamaeva Sloboda". This is a great opportunity to get to know the local culture, learn about the country's traditional craft, visit a mini-zoo, ride a horse-drawn carriage, watch performances of folk groups, buy some authentic Ukrainian souvenirs, and, of course, have a good time. Children would probably be interested in the State Museum of Toys where they can find out what kind of toys children who lived at different times played with. Those who'd prefer to learn more about the tragic milestones in the history of Ukraine are recommended to visit the Ukrainian National Chornobyl Museum and the Museum of the Great Patriotic War.

Attractions & nightlife

City break in Kiev. Active leisure ideas for Kiev attractions, recreation and nightlife

In addition to the variety of attractions, Kiev can offer hundreds of entertainment venues and night clubs, discos and sports complexes. City Entertainment center is located at the downtown. It offers a large number of great restaurants and a night club, a bowling club and a cozy hookah room with a river view, and a perfectly equipped nursery. Golf lovers have to visit GolfStream sport center, there would be interesting for both beginners and experienced players to spend a day. The sports complex has an equipment rental center, there is also an attractive restaurant and a great sports shop there.

Among other entertainment centers Olmeca Plage points out. In summer, it offers its visitors to relax on a beautiful beach and spend leisure-time in sports entertainment. The complex has several large swimming pools and a terrace with sun loungers and parasols. The stylish night club, national and Japanese food restaurants are always available for vacationers.

Fans of water rides will like the Terminal water park that provides a wide range of pools, rides, recreation areas and a café. The water park features a beautiful spa, several restaurants and bars, so the rest in it will appeal not only to children, but also for adults. It's also worth to visit Kiev dolphinarium; every day its pets arrange an enchanting show for guests. Visitors can take a picture with the dolphins and sea lions, swim in the pool with them and even try to feed.

Paradise Cabaret is a popular nightlife place. This popular cabaret, in addition to enchanting dance show, is preparing an interesting entertainment program for its guests. A fine restaurant and a hookah room are available for visitors. Among the city's discos it's worth to mention "Ultramarine" that is always ready for a great music program. Those who want a break from the noisy music will be able to move to the bar and try specialty cocktails. No less interesting is the nightlife of Docker Pub, this cozy pub welcomes guests every evening. It will be a great place to relax in a big company. There are also excellent shopping centers in Kiev, which can be found at every turn.

Kyiv is ready to offer hundreds of other opportunities - fans of active pastime will feel "like a fish in water" in the capital of Ukraine. Probably it would be easier to list what is not available here. Here you can fly a balloon over Kyiv's picturesque open spaces, do water sports - of course, in the summer (play beach volleyball and handball), ride a catamaran or boat, and even try snowboarding - this option is available in the winter time (Protasov Yar Sports Center). Thrill-seekers will be happy to jump with a parachute or visit one of the rope parks

(Seiklar, Sonyachny, in Troyeshchyna - the choice of parks is great) to get the most pleasant impressions from visiting the Ukrainian capital.

Butenko Stable located in a picturesque area offers its guests a wonderful leisure activity - riding graceful horses or ponies along a beautiful forest, as well as visiting a local restaurant with excellent cuisine. Horse or pony riding in "Favorit" Equestrian Club brings a lot of fun too. Among other things, here there are animals of completely different breeds, about which you can learn a lot of interesting things. Besides that, here is a mini-zoo with pigs, goats, and chickens on the territory. The Kyiv Zoo is a must-have, especially if you're traveling with small tourists. Here you can watch raccoons, giraffes, lions, elephants, bison, as well as ride a fairytale train.

Another mini-zoo can be found in Art Mall, and its name is "Strana Enotia" (Raccoon Land). Besides cute raccoons, here you can see rabbits, lemurs, peacocks, ponies. And since this is a petting zoo, it's allowed to hold and feed many animals. One more place worth visiting is Oceanarium "Morskaya Skazka" (Sea Fairy Tale), which is home to many sea inhabitants such as turtles, fish, starfish, jellyfish. The complex has three thematic halls designed accordingly. Dream Island Waterpark is very popular among tourists, including both families and those traveling without kids. Besides amazing slides, of great interest here is a bath complex, a spa zone, jacuzzi, swimming pools for every taste.

It's not a problem to go ice skating in summer. The thing is that in Kyiv you can find Katok Skating Rink. It is especially interesting to visit this sports center in the evening when the laser show is turned on. Those wishing to play mini-golf will be glad to visit "Cosmo Golf". The beautifully designed sports complex attracts hundreds of visitors to join the game. "Four-legged House" Cafe is in high demand among tourists and locals. As the name implies, cats reign supreme here. Excellent design, relaxed atmosphere, the opportunity to stroke beautiful purrers and dine in their company - that's what makes this anti-cafe so popular.

While in Kyiv, be sure to visit VR HUB Club to get a fantastic virtual experience. Here, visitors are provided with a variety of games - a virtual reality station, PlayStation games, board games. Bowling enthusiasts often visit Gulliver, while those who'd rather prefer billiards should think about Promenada Club. Many tourists note a wonderful bar located in the city center. In "Dom Master Class" you can attend one of the interesting concerts - and all this in an intimate setting ensuring relaxing and getting closer to musicians. Other interesting places include Kiev Art School where you can learn to draw and Robo School where visitors are told about how the technology works and offered to try to create a real robot.

A unique experience can be found in "Three After Midnight" Club. This is a special place where one can discover senses often ignored by people. And for this one needs only one thing - complete darkness. The complex has five interactive rooms quite familiar to every visitor but at the same time unusual due to loss of vision. This is something that stirs the interest of those looking for some unique experience. Escape rooms are also popular in Kyiv, and the best centers for this are Vzperti (Locked) and Pod Zamkom (Under the Lock). It is simply impossible to get poor impressions here, even if you are hardly a stranger to escape quests, you'll be delighted with non-trivial scenarios.

Ninja House is a great place for lovers of active pastime, as well as those who wish to master climbing to be able to ascent to the mountain pick as part of the tour in the future. Also, the city has every opportunity to spend time actively behind the wheel - you only need to contact "Need for Speed" Karting Center. Falcon Paintball Club is another great place for those wishing to get a strong adrenaline shot. Here you can try laser tag or paintball and later have a picnic in a friendly atmosphere. Well, those who want to improve accuracy should head to Ibis Shooting Club and have a great time here.

Cuisine & restaurants

Cuisine of Kiev for gourmets. Places for dinner best restaurants
It's not easy to choose the best one among hundreds of Kiev restaurants. Let's start the story about most attractive gastronomic points of interest with the review of national cuisine restaurants. The

attractive Varenichnaya #1 restaurant is decorated in the style of past centuries. The specialty of this place is vareniki (kind of dumplings). This popular national dish here is prepared in twenty variations. In addition to the favorite kind of dumplings, visitors can try interesting vegetable dishes and drinks.

A wide range of dishes of national cuisine are offered by O'Panas restaurant. Its present menu includes popular soups, meat dishes, and a variety of desserts. The Panska Vtiha restaurant will delight guests not only with a rich menu, but also with an interesting entertainment program. It has the unusual status of "folk restaurant" that's because regular entertainment program features the best dance and music groups from Kiev.

In Kiev, there are restaurants of different styles. The French Gorchitsa restaurant is popular among foreign visitors and locals. It has won recognition from loyal customers due to the excellent quality of food and reasonable prices. Fans of Italian cuisine are fond of another restaurant, Walter Rossit; there are many celebrities among its regular customers. Here you can try excellent risotto and pasta with seafood specialties and delicious desserts. Dishes are accompanied by popular Italian wines.

For those who want to taste the real Italian pizza, we can recommend the Napule restaurant. Pizza is the brand dish here. There are dozens of varieties of pizza in menu. Advocates a vegetarian diet, fans of meat dishes, and seafood lovers all of them would find something suitable. Napule would be great for families as it provides visitors with a special kids menu.

Marrakesh restaurant offers Moroccan cuisine to its guests. Space there is decorated with original oriental style; you can see gold-embroidered cushions and carpets everywhere. Such an atmosphere would be a nice addition to the meal and would distract from the everyday hustle and bustle. Among Asian restaurants it's worth to mention Grill Asia; the basis of its menu consists of dishes cooked on the grill. Visitors strongly admire restaurant's meat treats.

In Kyiv restaurants, it's worth trying popular traditional Ukrainian dishes. They serve delicious borsch with garlic donuts (pampushkas) as well as dumplings (varenyky), which is an indispensable dish on the menu of regional restaurants. Their diversity is simply amazing, dumplings are cooked with dozens of different fillings. There are very hearty varenyky with mushrooms, meat, and potatoes, while dessert options may include various fruits and berries. Before serving at the table, unsweetened dumplings are usually decorated with fried onions, sour cream or fresh herbs. For sweet dumplings, there is a special sugar syrup making the dish even sweeter.

Everyday dish for locals is jellied meat (kholodets), once it was cooked for the sole purpose of using up leftover meat. Today, the best meat products are selected for cooking kholodets. It is usually made from beef or pork legs. It is always customary to serve jellied meat with fresh bread and a special sauce from fresh horseradish or mustard.

Regional cuisine restaurants presented in Kyiv will certainly appeal to all fans of meat dishes. They prepare dozens of hearty meals of beef and pork, while poultry meat is much less frequently used in national cooking. A special menu item is local sausages, which can be tasted not only in local restaurants but also in local markets. Homemade sausages are most often prepared from pork. During the cooking, various spices are added to the mince to make the taste of sausages very rich.

Residents of Kiev are big fans of salo (cured slabs of fatback), which may serve as an independent product or a complement to various dishes. It can be stewed, fried, and even boiled. Salo is also used for the preparation of traditional garlic roll. Fans of unusual soups must try "Kulesh" in local restaurants. Many years ago, this original soup was cooked by the Zaporozhian Cossacks. Now its various recipes are popular in many regions of Ukraine. Compulsory components are cereals and salo, which are added to the soup just before serving. In addition to these components, various types of meat, seasonal vegetables and greens can also be used. Fans of desserts should pay special attention to sweet pastries in Kyiv restaurants.

Traditions & lifestyle

Colors of Kiev traditions, festivals, mentality and lifestyle
Travelers wishing to get acquainted with Kyiv's beautiful national traditions should visit the city during one of the major holidays. One of the favorite holidays among local residents is the City Day, which is traditionally celebrated on the last weekend of May. The tradition of celebrating this day appeared in 1982 and in recent years Kyiv Day has gained incredible scale. Sports competitions, the traditional balloons parade and concerts of popular performers are always held in Kyiv on holiday days.

No less interesting is the entertainment dedicated to arts and creativity. More than 30 years ago, the city began holding the so-called "vernissages" - art exhibitions, which have been held on Kyiv Day to this day. The best masters of the city present their masterpieces, any of which can be bought. Hand-embroidered aprons and colorful bedspreads, original handmade hats and jewelry, magnificent paintings and traditional costumes are just a small part of what Kyiv masters present for sale.

Local residents also celebrate numerous religious holidays, and the most famous one is St. Michael's Day. Celebrated on November 21, many customs associated with this holiday have remained unchanged over several hundred years. The holiday is dedicated to the main patron saint of Kyiv - Saint Michael the Archangel.

On this day, people avoid doing hard physical work and lay the table to spend the day with loved ones. On this holiday, it is also customary to please the "Dvorovoi", a spirit who is responsible for the courtyard and domestic order. To do this, one needs to leave it a glass of milk and a treat. Many of those who observe this ritual today note that by the morning the amount of milk in the glass is significantly reduced, which is a good sign.

Some of the most splendid celebrations and interesting entertainment are traditionally held in Kyiv on the days of Maslenitsa (Butter Week). The main symbol of this holiday is pancakes, which embody the sun and the long-awaited advent of spring. A large part of Maslenitsa's entertainment programs takes place in the open air.

Gastronomic festivals are organized on the squares, artists and musicians wearing beautiful national costumes perform on the streets, and the main final stage is the burning of Lady Maslenitsa. Besides public festivities, it is customary to observe some spiritual traditions on this day. On a holiday, people ask for forgiveness from loved ones, as well as clean away all bad thoughts.

Local residents are characterized by a very reverent and respectable attitude towards historical traditions. Beautiful national costumes, culinary specialties, traditional dances, and music are all mandatory attributes of any holiday. Among other typical traits of local people are thoroughness and deliberateness.

Whatever they need to do, locals will do everything without haste and very carefully. In many respects, Kyiv residents owe this national peculiarity to their beautiful national costumes. Their preparation for holidays begins long in advance; all national costumes are decorated with skillful handmade embroidery.

The pursuit of competition and leadership is another important trait of local people. This is the reason why hundreds of years ago all kinds of competitions have always been held in Kyiv on big holidays. Men could compete in fights and women in the art of cooking and needlework. Thus, all sorts of sports competitions are mandatory attributes of the holiday even today.

A striking character trait that is often perceived with misunderstanding is thrift and a negative attitude towards wastefulness. Such special features are perceived by many as greed, whereas in fact, it's just a manifestation of a caring attitude towards fruits of labor. Love for tasty and hearty food has always been an important component of the character of Kyivans. Here it is customary to set a rich table on any given holiday. However, even on a typical day, having a rich table is considered one of the main signs of wealth and well-being. One of the main ways of hospitality manifestation in Kyiv is an invitation to lunch or dinner. Refusing such offers may offend your hospitable Ukrainian friends. Kyivans respect and cherish their historical traditions and are always willing to let travelers from other cities and countries in on them.

Shopping in Kiev

Shopping in Kiev authentic goods, best outlets, malls and boutiques
Kyiv has a lot of interesting shopping malls. Dozens of product categories are presented in Globus Shopping Center. It houses clothing and footwear stores of various price categories, elite underwear and jewelry stores, and several other large sports shops. Ladies will be able to visit Women`secret store or boutiques of famous brands such as Springfield and Pierre Cardin. On the lower floor of the shopping center is a large food court area, and for budget travelers here is great Billa supermarket.

Even the whole day wouldn't be enough to explore all the shops of Dream Town Shopping and Entertainment Mall. Within its walls are boutiques of the most famous European brands, Bershka and Stradivarius shops, and United Colors for fans of bright fashionable clothes. Besides clothing and shoe stores, a number of interesting gastronomic pavilions operates in this mall. For example, Polyana store specializing in excellent wines. In terms of design, this shopping center is one of the most original and spectacular in town.

One of the largest malls not only in the city but in the country is Caravan. It has more than 200 shops, as well as about 20 restaurants and cafes, a cinema and a huge hypermarket. Thrifty customers will have the opportunity to visit O'STIN and Zara, and admirers of elite brands are provided with high-class boutiques like Marc O'Polo, Calzedonia, and Women'secret. This shopping center is perfect for visiting with children; here there are many shops full of children's clothes and toys.

Also, it's worth paying attention to amazing OCEAN PLAZA, which is located in the heart of Kyiv and occupies a spectacular building with a glass facade resembling a huge crystal from afar. This shopping mall offers 420 stores, it is second to none in terms of design and decoration in Kyiv. Here, shopping can be combined with admiring unique light installations. There are about three dozen restaurants and cafes in the shopping center. The mall has Converse and MEXX stores, while Cropp Town and LC Waikiki are popular among fans of youthful style. Auchan hypermarket can be found on the first floor, and the main feature of the shopping complex is a 350,000-liter aquarium, which is home to about a thousand exotic fish and other representatives of the underwater world.

Continue searching for new fashionable outfits and accessories in SKYMALL - it is especially popular among young people. The mall houses 260 stores, including boutiques from New Yorker, Topshop, and Warehouse. Ladies will love huge cosmetic store Bonjour where they can pick decorative cosmetics from leading world brands and chic perfume. Besides that, SKYMALL has the largest children's toy store in town - PLANETTOYS supermarket. A huge play area is equipped in the mall for the youngest visitors.

Those who are used to shopping at the most expensive and sophisticated stores would probably be interested in visiting Cosmopolite MULTIMALL. There are no budget stores here, all salons and boutiques are focused on customers with above-average incomes. The mall will appeal to fans of brands such as Geox and Northland, as well as exquisite designer boutiques like Karen Millen and Tally Weijl. Many people visit the mall for the sake of Yamaha music store selling musical instruments and accessories from the world's best manufacturers.

Lovers of walks through Kyiv's colorful markets must visit the Bessarabian Market. This market presents all possible categories of popular products, ranging from meat and fish delicacies to delicious oriental sweets, exotic fruits, and vegetables. The indoor market occupies a beautiful historic building. In addition to stalls, it has several mini-cafes where you can buy some popular street food at cheap prices.

Tips for tourists

Preparing your trip to Kiev: advices & hints things to do and to obey
1. The most profitable way is to pay for goods and services with national currency; you can use an exchange in any bank of the city.

Most banks are open 5 days a week; Saturday and Sunday are days-off. Some large banks serve customers on Saturdays.

2. Tap water is not recommended to drink; it's better to purchase purified bottled water, which you can buy at any grocery store. In Kiev there are lots of pumprooms, all decorated in style of antique hand pumps, they can be found in the territory of any park. You can take the purest artesian water there without any fee.

3. The city has a ban on smoking in public places, but special areas for smoking are ubiquitous. In restaurants and bars hall is often divided into two parts, one of which is intended for those who smoke, and the other for non-smoking ones.

4. Public transport is represented in Kiev in all possible forms. The most convenient way is to move around the city by subway, which runs from 6:00 am to 12:00pm. From early morning until late at night taxis and buses, as well as trams and trolley buses convenient for traveling short distances, are cruising through the streets.

5. Tourists, who expect to visit restaurants of national cuisine, have to consider that menu there changes every season. Chefs use only seasonal vegetables and organic foods for cooking, that's why they are so popular.

6. In large restaurants a service charge may be included in the overall bill. If the item is not provided in the bill, then you can add about 5 -

10% of the total amount. It is also appropriate to leave tips for the taxi driver and guides.

7. Main voltage is 220V; many hotels have standard European type socket. Be sure to specify these nuances in advance when booking your room to pick up necessary adapters.

8. Staff at the luxury hotels, upscale restaurants and shopping complexes is fluent in foreign languages. However, in many places menu can be provided only in Ukrainian, so feel free to ask waiters about things you concern.

9. It is advisable to take a copy of an identity document with you, when you go for a walk. Travelers, who visit Kiev for the first time, are encouraged to take the tourist office map of the city. This will make walking around even more simple and enjoyable

Koktebel

Guide to Koktebel

Sightseeing in Koktebel what to see. Complete travel guide
Koktebel belongs to the category of those cities whose foundation date is not known. The history of Koktebel is covered with a veil of mystery and has hardly been studied, and there are almost no archaeological monuments of its past. It is known that in the territory of the modern city, there used to be a fairly large medieval fortified settlement, which soon became a successful commercial sea port.

However, the valleys of Karadag, near which Koktebel is located, have been inhabited for a long time. Here lived the Cimmerians, and then the Taurians and Scythians, as well as natives of the Bosporus, destroyed by the barbarians.

In the 10th century the Pechenegs destroyed the city completely, and life in it resumed only after several centuries. After that there was a small Tatar village, and then a Bulgarian settlement. Until the end of the 19th century it was a small town through which an important road passed to Feodosia. At the beginning of the 20th century, in a picturesque and quiet city, the literary elite and other representatives of bohemia began to settle; they bought plots in the Koktebel Valley and built luxurious mansions.

Many famous people visited Koktebel, but most often the village is associated with the name of Maximilian Voloshin, the famous poet of the Silver Age. The outstanding artist and poet became the soul of Koktebel; it was he who found here the ruins of an ancient settlement. Voloshin loved this place for its pristine and wild beauty. He is buried in Koktebel, at the very top of the Kuchuk-Yenishar Mountain, which is located very near the Cape Chameleon. The poet himself wished to be buried there, and also asked that trees and flowers not be planted near his grave, as he loved Koktebel in his natural beauty.

Maximilian Voloshin did a lot for Koktebel and does, probably still, even after his death. The house where he lived became a museum, and very many people come here to see pictures of the famous poet and artist, who at one time, was visited by many outstanding personalities. Slowly but surely the village developed, and in the 30s of the last century there were already seven large holiday homes. The Great Patriotic War negatively affected the life of the village; during the war Koktebel was almost completely empty. Now Koktebel is one of the popular holiday destinations on the Crimean coast, as well as a permanent venue for a beautiful jazz festival.

The guests of the famous resort have an opportunity to visit the Karadag Natural Reserve. Its main attraction is the Karadag Mountain Range that is nothing but a huge extinct volcano. Millions of years ago, multiple eruptions impacted the formation of the special natural landscape. Some parts of the reserve really impress with its desert lunar landscapes. Near them, you can see vast green valleys. The reserve sharply contracts with natural landscapes.

Those who want to learn more details about the features of the natural reserve should visit the Karadag Nature Museum located in the surroundings of Koktebel. In 1914, the scientific base was created in this area. Its biological artifacts are a core of the museum exposure. Now, among thousands of exhibits, you can see stuffed birds and rare animals, species of rare plants and insects, and a lot of other themed exhibits dedicated to flora and fauna of the reserve.

Another interesting natural object is the rock that was called Golden Gate for its unusual arched shape. The beautiful rock protrudes from the sea not far from the coast. It is more interesting to admire it in the sun. You can visit this unique attraction in the context of the excursion around the reserve. You can also take a boat trip to the rock.

Koktebel is primarily known as a beach resort. The total length of its beaches is about 4 000 m. The resort attracts more tourists in June and August. Fans of water entertainments have an opportunity to visit the local waterpark that is one of the largest in the region. It occupies almost 44 000 m2. In the waterpark, there are 7 pools, over 20 slides, and a lot of interesting water attractions. There are also special recreation areas and attractions for children of different ages. In the middle of the tourist season, the waterpark is visited by over a thousand people every day.

The dolphinarium where you can watch performances with different sea dwellers will impress you too. Besides dolphins, you can see here popular whales and sea bears. The dolphinarium of Koktebel has recently taken an active part in topical environmental programs.

Culture: sights to visit

Culture of Koktebel. Places to visit old town, temples, theaters, museums and palaces
Koktebel is a fairly compact city, so it does not have a lot of attractions. The magnificent bay in the embrace of the volcano

Karadag, the mountains of Uzup-Syrt and the range of Kiik Atlama are the most important symbols of the resort city and priceless natural places of interest. Resting in Koktebel, it is necessary to visit the house of Maximilian Voloshin, in which he spent the best creative years of his life. Here you can see the magnificent watercolors of the poet and his friend, the artist Bogaevsky. It is also interesting to visit the top of the Kuchuk-Yenishar Mountain, where the poet is buried.

Of the tourist sites, the Gliding Museum on Mount Klementyev is noteworthy, where Korolev himself, the famous creator of spaceships, once lifted gliders into the sky. One of the most loved and visited places are the winery, on the territory of which there are daily interesting excursions. The main winery is on a hill in which tunnels for wine storage have been dug at two levels. The total length of the tunnels is more than one and a half kilometers. This is where the largest wine-growing area in Europe is located and where the delicious Maderia is produced. The factory specializes in the production of vintage wines, so it will be of interest to collectors.

The most important natural attraction is the volcano Karadag which according to historical data, was more than 150 million years old. Currently, the volcano is in the territory of a vast nature reserve. When speaking about it, usually remember another masterpiece of nature-the Golden Gate. It is called so because it is located near the foot of the volcano formation which in appearance resembles a huge gate.

In addition to natural and historical attractions, Koktebel is interesting with its unique monuments. One of the most beautiful sculptural compositions is on the waterfront. It is dedicated to the victims of the Great Patriotic War. The picturesque city with a mysterious history does not cease to attract the attention of adherents of excursion tourism. The main part of its sightseeing facilities is natural monuments, whose value is also high, as well as outstanding historical sites.

Attractions & nightlife

City break in Koktebel. Active leisure ideas for Koktebel attractions, recreation and nightlife
Opportunities for active recreation in Koktebel are incredibly much. Those who do not want to rest on the beach can spend a lot of exciting excursions to charming places. Everyone can go on an exciting trip for a few days, and fully appreciate the beauty of nature. Koktebel has long been a recognized center of paragliding, and parachutists like to rest here. Jumps are made with a parachute system "Wing" at an altitude of 1200 meters. Everyone can go through preliminary training, then make a jump and get a parachutist certificate. However, for this you need to jump with a parachute at least three times.

On Mount Klementyev, where the Museum of Gliding is located, you can learn to fly on a paraglide. Those who are still afraid to fly on their own, are offered a more "sparing" kind of entertainment, they can fly on a paraglide along with an instructor. Travelers who have long dreamed of trying themselves in the role of an airplane pilot will have such an opportunity in Koktebel. Absolutely all after full instruction can fly on a super-maneuverable plane over the Crimea, performing aerobatics figures and independently controlling the aircraft.

Travelers, who are attracted by the unknown depths of the Crimean Mountains, can go on foot on the plateau of Karabi Yayla - the largest and deserted plateau in the Crimea. Here you can see the cave of Studencheskoy, in which the rock paintings are preserved, as well as the cave Bolshaya Buzluk, whose depth is 81 meters. Those who do not like walking, will have the opportunity to ride on the mountain valleys of the Crimea on first-class jeeps. Practicing in Koktebel rope-jumping - jumping from the cliff on the insurance. This entertainment will appeal to fans of extreme sports.

Fans of beach recreation in addition to the picturesque coast should pay attention to the water park of Koktebel, which is considered the best in the region. It occupies a vast territory and is well-equipped, so you can relax here comfortably even on the hottest day. On the evening walk it is best to go to the embankment, and for memorable gifts for loved ones - to one of the city markets. The Central Market has the largest choice of goods. Nightlife in Koktebel is concentrated on the embankment. In addition to local discos and nightclubs, an interesting evening program is offered to visitors of the "Calypso" or "La Boheme café".

Cuisine & restaurants

Cuisine of Koktebel for gourmets. Places for dinner best restaurants
As in many resort towns, the gastronomic life of Koktebel is mainly concentrated on its embankment. In the morning and in the afternoon you can easily have a snack or order a complex dinner. On the waterfront there are attractive cheap institutions and more prestigious restaurants. In the evening, modest cafes are transformed into real entertainment centers with an interesting show program and a top-level service. Those who prefer to cook on their own, trusting only their own skill, should go to the grocery market. Here you can buy both the necessary products, and already cooked meals. The choice of grocery stores and supermarkets in the resort is also very large.

For economical travelers, a real find will be numerous cafes and restaurants, which offer pretty high-quality fast food. A huge selection of such institutions is situated on the "Desantnikov Street", as well as on the waterfront. In attractive restaurants you can order hot dogs or hot sandwiches, drink beer and try several kinds of pizza. It is worth noting that the pizza in Koktebel is simply excellent, experienced culinary experts prepare it in different variants.

For those who do not like fast food establishments, it is worth paying attention to the classic cafeterias, which in the town are also many. The food in them is very tasty and quite cheap. Some popular cafeterias are perfect for visiting with children. From the huge variety of institutions of this level, it is worth highlighting the cafeteria "Lozhka", which is located on the waterfront. Not far from the central market is the cafeteria "Rybka", in which those who are not indifferent to the dishes from the seafood will especially like to rest. From simple and affordable fish, local chefs prepare incredibly tasty treats.

Those who wish to get acquainted with the classical gastronomy of a picturesque resort should pay attention to one of the Tatar restaurants. Visitors to them must be offered an attractive shish kebab, chebureks, pilaf, samsa, shurpa and lagman. The interior of such institutions is always sustained in national traditions; its invariable attributes are luxurious carpets and pillows. The restaurant of national cuisine "Emine" is located right on the beach; it has long won recognition among fans of shish kebab and a foamy drink.

Koreiz

Guide to Koreiz

Sightseeing in Koreiz what to see. Complete travel guide
Koreiz is a wonderful resort village located 12 km from enchanting Yalta. The boundaries of Koreiz and Gaspra have long mingled and only the indigenous people can say where one village ends and

another starts. In Russian literature, this picturesque Crimean village was first mentioned by academician P. S. Pallas. He traveled to these beautiful places in 1793-1794. A little later, Koreiz was visited by academician P. I. Sumarokov. On the basis of information from the Lists of Populated Areas of the Russian Empire, there were about 25 palaces in Koreiz in 1865. They were inhabited by 130 people. Also, there was a working mosque and a post office with two yards and 15 residents in the village.

In the late 19th century, Koreiz became a peculiar capital of surrounding cities, towns, villages and villa quarters. In 1914, there was a telegraph, a telephone station, a post office, pharmacy, a coffee house, wine shops, and other venues characterizing big cities. Since 1785, G. A. Potemkin had started actively encouraging the development of horticulture and viniculture in Crimea. He invited specialists and imported the best grapes. After the Crimean War, the southern coast was very attractive for landlords, noble people, and high royal officials.

The village was being built up by different hotels, restaurants, private guest houses, and gambling houses that attracted adherents of beautiful leisure to these places. The construction involved legendary architects and engineers. Koreiz has turned into a luxurious aristocratic resort within just a few years.

One of the first landlords' residences on the territory of the village is a mansion built in the 20s of the 19th century by Duchess A. A. Golitsyna. After some time, duke Yusupov bought this mansion. In 1904, the palace in the modern style was built under the project of Yalta architect N. P. Krasnov. When the Yalta Conference was held in 1945, exactly the Yusupov Palace accommodated the entire Soviet delegation. Modern Koreiz seems very attractive to fans of ecotourism and those who prefer calm and peaceful resorts. This enchanting village with its unique history and atmosphere where you can enjoy the harmony of the world around you, walk along picturesque places, and taste the best Crimean wines.

Despite its tiny area, the resort will impress fans of sightseeing tours with multiple attractions. The most beautiful architectural monument is the Dulber Palace built for the royal family in 1897. When it was finished, Peter Nikolayevich Romanov, the uncle of Emperor Nicholas II, lived here. After the Revolution, the sanatorium was opened here. It is still working now. The landscape garden surrounding the palace is very popular too.

In the picturesque park, there is the Kichkine Palace. It was built in 1913. The palace belonged to Dmitriy Konstantinovich Romanov. The historical monument was built in the Eastern style and decorated with sophisticated carved towers and domes. Its facade is decorated with arches and patterns. Several years ago, the hotel was opened in this historical palace. Today, everyone can spend several days in this picturesque atmosphere of the past.

Nature admirers also like walking along submontane areas of Ai-Petri. The mountain is distinguished by many caves on its slopes. There are over 300 caves here. Only some of them are open for visitors. The most interesting cave is called Trehglazka. Its unique feature is its microclimate. The air temperature here is quite low during the year. The visitors have an opportunity to see a big snowdrift and cave lake covered with ice. The ice in the cave doesn't melt even in hot weather.

If you don't want to go far from the resort to admire incredible landscapes, you should visit the Chair Park. It is very beautiful and presents the rich collection of rare tropical plants. Here, you can see different types of cypresses. There is also a big rose garden in the park. The Chair Park is a historic site. It was founded in the late 19th century. Today, you can see here trees aged over a hundred years. It will be also very interesting for fans of beach recreation to visit Koreiz. Almost all local hotels and guesthouses are located in the well-equipped coastal area.

Livadiya

Guide to Livadiya

Sightseeing in Livadiya what to see. Complete travel guide

In ancient times, there were big meadows at the site of the modern resort. So, many people thought that Livadia got its name exactly because of its relief, as the Greek word "livadion" means "lawn, meadow". The territory of Livadia had long been settled, which is proved by the remains of the settlements of the Copper Age found by archeologists near Oreanda. They date back to the 3rd century BC. The researchers also found the remains of the Taurus settlement and the burial site near it that date back to the 1st century BC. The remains of pottery found here and the medieval settlement with the burial site and the cathedral confirm the fact that people lived here in the 8th-9th centuries.

The ruins of the feudal castle found on Mount Hachla Kayasy that date back to the 10th-11th centuries have survived to this day. In the 18th century, there was a small Greek settlement at the site of present Livadia. It was called Ay Yan after St. John. Upon the order of the king, its residents moved to the Azov Governorate in the second half of the 18th century.

After Crimea coming to the Russian Empire, most of the lands on the Southern bank was distributed to the Greek soldiers of the Balaklav battalion that protected the Crimean borders at that time. Later, battalion commander Theodosius Reveliotis bought the best lands including Livadia from his soldiers. In the 30s of the 19th century, the prices for these lands rose sharply, which was mostly caused by the laying of the new road connecting Yalta with Simferopol and Sevastopol.

In 1834, Livadia was bought by a Polish tycoon, count Lev Pototsky. At the end of the 30s, he put up the vineyard here. In 1860, his square was almost 19 hectares. Wine has started being produced since that time. Also, the big wine cellar for storing wines was built. Over two thousand buckets and four thousand buckets of wine were produced in 1848 and 1853 respectively. At that time, a church, two manor houses, outbuildings and residential buildings were constructed here. In 1859, there were thirty palaces in Livadia where about 150 people lived. Livadia was constantly expanding. It turned from a small village to a beautiful city that today attracts inquisitive tourists with its beauty and cultural wealth.

The irreplaceable symbol of the historical resort is the Livadia Palace. It was built in 1834 upon the order of the emperor Nicholas II. For the years of its existence, this wonderful palace has been rebuilt for many times. It was destroyed completely in 1909. Then, it was restored in accordance with the first projects. After the Revolution of 1917, the prestigious sanatorium was opened in 1917and only high politicians could vacation here. Today, the palace serves as the Museum of Architecture. Everyone can admire its luxurious interior and walk through the garden surrounding the palace.

The Livadia Park is considered as an independent attraction. Today, it occupies almost 40 hectares. The park is thoroughly cared for. Over 400 plant species are presented here. In the park, you can walk along beautiful oleander alleys and see evergreen bushes and trees that are typical for local nature. Not so long ago, over 7 000 rosebushes were planted in the territory of the park. It is very interesting to visit the park during the blooming period.

Several years ago, the Inverted House was opened in Livadia. It is a small house turned upside down. In this unusual house, all pieces of furniture are turned upside down. Every day, this unusual attraction is visited by curious tourists who want to take spectacular pictures.

In Livadia, there are a lot of unique nature attractions, among which the wonderful waterfall Uchan Su is worth being mentioned. It is the highest waterfall on the Crimean peninsula. It is 390 m high. The waterfall is "fed" by glaciers, so it reaches its greatness in the spring. It is located in a very beautiful mountainous. Hiking tour to the waterfall may turn into an unforgettable adventure. Diving fans will have an opportunity to see the unique sea attraction. There is the tug "Baikal" lying in the coastal waters. It sank here during the storm in 1969 and still lies on the sea bottom.

Lviv
Guide to Lviv

Sightseeing in Lviv what to see. Complete travel guide
Lvov is a magnificent place. This is one of the richest cities of Ukraine in terms of architecture and culture. Lvov is widely known in Europe. It is even called "pearl" of Eastern Europe due to its uniqueness and beauty. Lvov conquers even most hard-to-please visitors and tourists keep the memories of it long after the visit.

Travellers will find numerous architectural monuments, museums, theaters, ancient churches in Lvov. Everything here is simply soaked in uniqueness. There are also many cafes and restaurants that are located right on the crossing cobbled streets of the city. Among the main sights of this place are Lvov Opera House, Gunpowder Tower, City Hall on Market Square, the Dominican church, Lychakiv cemetery and many other attractions and sights.

In the old part of city is located Market Square. All four sides of the square are surrounded by 44 houses referring to different styles and periods (Baroque, Renaissance, Empire). These buildings have undergone numerous restorations and renovations, but their cellars have retained the elements of Gothic architecture of XV-XVI centuries. Lychakiv cemetery, which was founded in 1786, is known as a historical and memorial museum complex featuring works of famous architects and sculptors. Tourists may certainly find much interesting in visiting Shevchekovsky gai, Pharmacy-Museum, the city arsenal, research library, kostels and churches. Here are also located museums dedicated to art, history, brewing, ethnography, ancient Ukrainian books, and more. In order to get acquainted with the real Ukrainian spirit, you should definitely visit the underground of Lvov, as well as get some rest cafes and restaurants decorated in ethnic style.

An outstanding architectural monument is the Potocki Palace. At the end of the 19th century, it belonged to a wealthy count family. This palace was built in 1880, by famous Polish architects. The unique architectural appearance of the magnificent palace is preserved. The palace is surrounded by a flourishing garden, so many prefer to visit the architectural monument in the warm season.

The historical facility of an earlier period is the Korniakt Palace, which is considered a true example of the Renaissance style. The palace was built in the 16th century for a wealthy Greek merchant, whose name he still bears. At the time of completion of the construction, this palace was officially considered the most luxurious in the city. Among its main features is the charming Italian courtyard. By design, it is very similar to the classic patio, which can be seen in Florence. Now in the palace, there is a museum as well as a restaurant. In summer, part of its tables is served in the courtyard.

A very interesting historical site is the House of Scientists, which was built in one of the central streets of Lviv, back in the late 19th century. Originally, in this spectacular building, the entrance to which is decorated with sculptures in antique style, was located a casino. In

1948, the beautiful building was occupied by one of the organizations of the educational sphere, in whose charge the building is now.

Among the religious monuments of Lviv, is the St. George's Cathedral. It was built in the 14th century on the site of a destroyed old church. This cathedral is a fairly large architectural complex with beautiful terraces, a garden, as well as the Metropolitan's Palace and chapter's house.

One of the most unusual and impressive is the Armenian Cathedral. It was also built in the 14th century and is located in the historic district of the city. In the 12th century, the old Armenian Church was located, on the spot where the cathedral was built. Now the medieval cathedral attracts tourists with its incredible decoration. Elements of medieval art, interesting religious artifacts and jewelry made of wood, are preserved in it.

Admirers of unusual excursions should go to the Lontsky Street, where the old prison is located. Until 1991, there was a pre-trial detention center here and in 2009, an interesting thematic museum was opened in its building. The exhibits of the museum are housed directly in old prison cells.

Family trip with kids

Family trip to Lviv with children. Ideas on where to go with your child

In Lviv, tourists with children just do not have to be bored. Many of them start the excursion program with a visit to the zoo "Limpopo". This zoo has a collection of animals from all over the world. You can see the main representatives of the animal world of Africa including lions and cheetahs. Aviaries with lemurs and raccoons are particularly popular amongst visitors with young children. Visitors are allowed to feed many friendly zoo inhabitants. On the territory of the zoo, there is an excellent terrarium in which you can see exceptional species of snakes and a special aviary prepared for exotic birds.

The water park "Beach" remains a favorite location for fans of water sports. It is an indoor water park, so you can visit it at any time of the year. This water park is largely centered on visitors with children. It has a unique pool for kids and colorful slides of varying complexity. There are also stunning relaxation areas with sun loungers in the water park and a relaxation area with Jacuzzi and sauna that is sure to delight adults.

For those who would love the whole family to go to the movies, it is worth visiting one of the most modern and famous cinemas in Lviv "Planeta Kino". It offers its visitors several first-class colorful cinemas. It would not be difficult to choose a movie for family viewing in this cinema. There is a large lovely cafe with artistic illumination, as well as several magnificent relaxation areas with upholstered furniture in the cinema.

Fitting entertainment can be found for vacationers with young children. They should definitely visit the children's club "Lys Mikita". Here playgrounds and recreation areas are prepared for children from the age of two years. In the center, there are cutting-edge slides, inflatable attractions and trampolines. Also, thrilling entertainment programs are organized for young visitors. They can become participants in theatrical performances, play active games and take part in fascinating workshops.

A vacation in Lviv with children must be diversified by visiting popular parks. One of the most picturesque is "Stryi Park". In the center of this well-kept park, there is a large lake in which swans live. The favorite leisure for many regular visitors remains feeding the swans. There are many recreation spots with benches and spacious paths within the park, and several interesting monuments on its territory. This park is ideal for cycling. Also, many pet squirrels which children will also like live in the park.

Another picturesque place that is perfect for family walks is the Botanical Garden of Lviv University. The garden is particularly attractive in the warm season, when many flowers and landscape compositions are planted on its territory. In this park, there are always many vacationers with children. Even in autumn, it is very stunning here and you can see a number of extraordinary ornaments.

The most eye-catching museum for children in Lviv is the Chocolate Museum. It is far more like an original entertainment center where there are very interesting workshops and cognitive excursions for visitors. In this museum, everyone will be able to learn how to prepare chocolate from cocoa beans and also try scrumptious chocolate desserts. On the territory of the museum, there is an elegant café-confectionery. Some of the chocolate products presented in it resemble real works of art.

Culture: sights to visit
Culture of Lviv. Places to visit old town, temples, theaters, museums and palaces
The best part of city sights is concentrated in the central district of the city. Rambling is the best way for tourists to explore the historic area of the city of Lvov. Tourists should better start sightseeing from the railway station. The ancient building with its delicate arch covering is of greatest majesty and beauty. The architectural landmark is better viewed from the platform. The way from the railway station to the city center takes only few minutes. The first city sight on the way will be the Kropivnitsky Square and the Church of St. Olha and Elizabeth.

Being the best incarnation of the Neo-Gothic Architecture the church by its form resembles a traditional French construction. Another object of touristic interest is the St. Yura Cathedral being a scaled architectural complex built in the Rococo style. The church is the

160

global scale landmark and is considered to be the most impressive building of the city. The religious building is located in the Ozarkevich street which is famous for its numerous historical constructions.

The Lvov Opera House will be of great interest not only for theater lovers but for admirers of ancient architecture. The Lvov Opera House is considered to be one of the best in Europe. In front of the Opera House a small court is equipped. The court features fountains and flower beds. The building of the Lvov City Hall should be undoubtedly included in the tour. One of the towers of historical building is now equipped with a spacious viewing platform which offers a precise scene of the city with its landmarks and monuments.

Freedom Avenue (or Prospect Svobody) is a perfect place for hiking. The prospect hosts two significant monuments. One of them is dedicated to Taras Shevchenko, and another one is devoted to Adam Mitskevich. The scenic prospect will guide the city guests to the religious landmark the Lvov's Latin Cathedral. Among other architectural landmarks the High Castle is worth of greatest attention. Its name totally explains the peculiarity of its look. Among the Medieval constructions the most noticeable are the Royal Armory and the powder tower. Nowadays the buildings of the Royal Armory are hosing the Armory Museum

Attractions & nightlife

City break in Lviv. Active leisure ideas for Lviv attractions, recreation and nightlife

Upscale nightclubs, shopping and entertainment centers, scale markets, scenic parks and large sport complexes are the minor part of the entertainments Lvov offers to its visitors. Enthusiasts of billiards and bowling should pay a visit to the Barkley pub. Its visitors can set comfortably in the cozy hall or at the bar counter and order favorite beer and thereafter to proceed to the playing hall and devote some time to favorite game. The fans of contemporary music and dancing will better like the Cult nightclub located in the ancient cellar under the building of Lvov Philharmonic. Daily the visitors of the place are offered exciting parties and entertaining shows.

Another renowned night spot is the Chocolate Bar. Apart from a vast selection of speciality drinks and sweet treats the place offers to its guests a rich entertaining program. The bar engages popular music bands and DJs to keep the public hot. The local carting center is the same worth attention. It will turn to a perfect place of family leisure.

The nature enthusiasts will surely love the Botanical garden located on the territory of the National Forestry Engineering University of Ukraine. Its vast territory is a perfect place to walk and enjoy the sights of exotic plants and fragrant flowers. The history of the Lvov Botanical Garden dates back to the beginning of the by-gone century. Each year its vast collection of plants is added with ever new exotic specimens. The great choice of parks in Lvov will stun those tourists giving preference to outdoor recreation. Zamarstynovky park, the woodland park "Zubra", Lewandowsky park and Bruchovichisky park are the few of natural areas which will best fit as for sport entertainments, so for picnics.

The city has more than twenty parks and gardens each of them being charming, unique and glorious. In the evenings the guests are invited to visit the city cinemas. The 5D Cinema is of greatest popularity among city guests and local residents. The Kiev Cinema is the best to visit for watching some new films. Among the most popular cinemas there are also Sokol and Lvov. The best place for family visit is the entertaining center "Bez Problem" being of immense popularity among the youngest travelers. For older tourists the entertaining complex "Mi100" is the best leisure alternative. The complex offers as stylish bars and upscale restaurants so high end night clubs.

Cuisine & restaurants

Cuisine of Lviv for gourmets. Places for dinner best restaurants
Travelers wishing to try the dishes of Ukrainian cuisine in their genuine design and recipe should set off to the Veronika restaurant. This is a romantic and cozy inn featuring its own sweetshop. Daily the Veronika restaurant is visited by sweets' addicts as this is the only place where one can try chef's desserts.

A rich selection of European cuisine dishes is presented in the Culinary Studio Kryva Lypa. Guests will be stunned with the vast choice of salads, fish and meat dishes, refreshing drinks and delicious desserts. This budgetary inn will be a perfect place for a family visit. A full diner of three courses will cost about 15 Euro. One of the most romantic eating places of Lvov is considered to be Bianco Rosso Pasteria. The Italian cuisine is in the heart of its menu, however the chef's specialities are of immense popularity among the guests of the house too. The restaurant will be a perfect place as for a romantic date and so for festive events.

Those wishing to enjoy the casual atmosphere and the delicious local cuisine treats will better like the Kryjivka restaurant. Perfect cheap dinners at attractive prices, spacious and fine decorated hall, an impressive selection of ethnic dishes and high quality service are the main advantages of the popular eating place. The Kryjivka restaurant serves the visitors till the late night, tables for dinner are recommended to reserve in advance.

Another gastronomy landmark of Lvov being of immense popularity among city guests is the Kumpel restaurant which is set not fat from the city center. Its speciality is considered to be pelmeni (or meat pockets) which are traditionally added with special sauces with spice. The Amadeus restaurant serves the dishes of ethnic cuisine. Its interior is beset in historical style. In the daytime the main visitors of the place are the employees of the neighboring offices and tourists. To find a free table in the evening is a real challenge. Svit kavy is the best place to have a cup of savory coffee and to try some hot pastry. In the warm season the visitors can set on the spacious terrace. In cool weather the tables are served in a cozy hall.

Traditions & lifestyle

Colors of Lviv traditions, festivals, mentality and lifestyle
Lvov is an ancient city of unique cultural traditions and of unspeakable charming beauty. Annually the local people enjoy numerous exciting events and fests. The Annual City Beer Festival, the Day of Batyar, the Annual Wine and Cheese Fest, the feast of pampukh are the most exciting events. Apart of these the city presents events for true music lovers, the fans of gastronomic tourism and for those wishing to enjoy city culture and get some unique souvenirs.

Annually the city of Lvov is visited by thousands of beer fans. During the Annual City Beer Festival anybody gets a chance not only to try the best sorts of beer but to find out the secrets of its brewing. Within the event great many of exhibitions, lectures and master-classes are held. Expert brewers eagerly share their experience with the public. Another exciting national feast is the Day of Batyar. In the middle of 19th century the batyars were called the street artists performing in the streets of the city the exciting and bright music and dancing shows.

The culture of street artists was a marked contrast to that one characteristic to the edge of the 19th 20th centuries. Rhythmic music and dancing, original suits and unusual themes of the songs, audacious humor and untranslatable pun have always attracted to the performances many visitors. The batyars or the musician-humorists are still among the main symbols of Lvov. Tourists wishing to get to know the batyars and their culture better should visit Lvov in the beginning of May. The main festive events are held on the Lvov Market Square.

The name of the Annual Wine and Cheese Fest speaks for itself this is a genuine paradise for gourmands. The cheese is one of the most favorite ethnic delicacies. Local cheese factories produce the special cheese sorts following the ancient recipes. Regardless of the fact that Lvov does not rate now among significant wine-producing areas, the wine is still the favorite drink of local people. The golden age of Lvov winemaking fell at the end of the 17th century. Then the largest part of the city was occupied with vineyards. As a renowned merchant center Lvov attracted international producers thus local people got the rarest sorts of European wines for sale.

In course of time the climate of the city changed and the vineyards ceased cropping as before however the local folks have preserved the passion to the exquisite wine. In their opinion neither food except cheese can help accentuate the taste and flavor of astonishing wines. The feast of pampukh is the same exiting gastronomy fest being totally dedicated to the ethnic treat the pampushki (or Russian donuts).

Tips for tourists

Preparing your trip to Lviv: advices & hints things to do and to obey

1. Smoking tourists should take into account that local trains and buses are non smoking. For violating the smoking ban one will be charged with fees. One should pay attention to the restrictive signs placed in the streets. As a rule, near the government bodies and public establishments there are specially equipped smoking areas.

2. Lvov is a perfect destination for prudent tourists as the city offers a great variety of comfortable hostels. The hostel accommodation will cost from 10 to 15 euro per night. Many hostels are scattered around the city center.

3. Local restaurants also feature attractive pricing, the budgetary eating places are set at every turn. As a rule the upscale restaurants are placed in close vicinity of landmarks and monuments, the remote areas of the city will stun the guests with a selection of cafés, bars and pubs.

4. The time constrained tourists may be recommended to make a city tram tour. Almost every tram route goes through the significant places and landmarks of the city. The tram trip will turn into exciting experience. The tram ticket should be bought directly from the tram driver, then the ticket should be clipped.

5. The main transport means in Lvov is taxi. Tourists first visiting the city are recommended to call for official taxi services as this will help to specify the pricing. Then one can call for private taxi services which will cost 30 to 50% less than official services charge. However the unaware tourists may be charged with higher rates.

6. One should undoubtedly visit one of the touristic centers. One of them is placed directly near the railway station. Tourists will be offered a vast choice of guides and city maps which will turn of great help for every tourist.

7. Local people are respectful towards city guests however they give preference to the native language. Tourists should learn several phrases in Ukrainian as it will show their respectful attitude towards local people and will set connections with them.

8. The shopping addicts will be stunned with pricing in local shopping centers and boutiques. The prices are lower than in other cities of the country. At the same time the quality of the goods is still rather high. Souvenirs and promotional gifts should better be bought on the markets meanwhile trendy outfits and elite perfumes should better be bought in upscale shopping centers.

Odessa

Guide to Odessa
Sightseeing in Odessa what to see. Complete travel guide

Several years ago the city celebrated its two hundredth birthday. It was founded in 1794 by order of Catherine II. Odessa has always been the main port city of the Black Sea coast. Tourists are attracted by the city's good traditions and hospitality, beautiful architecture and spacious beaches.

There are really many places for walking in the city, and you can study its streets indefinitely. Here you will find beautiful old mansions and magnificent modern buildings, as well as numerous monuments and fountains. The old part of the city and its main symbol is the Deribasovskaya Street, along which is stretched a large square. Here you will see contemporary artists who show off their works; take a walk among the ancient sculptures and watch beautiful pictures of marine landscapes, portraits and still life pictures.

St. Panteleimon Monastery decorated with fine mosaics and five gleaming domes is one of the city's main attractions. You should definitely walk along the port area, which looks more like a modern city street rather than an old port. There are many modern buildings here, which feature a skillful mix of metal and glass. The Catacombs are one of the main historical monuments of Odessa. This is a real underground city, which complex labyrinth stretches for many kilometers underground. Attending the Catacombs can be done with a guide only, because the tunnels are very complicated and it's really easy to get lost in them.

Odessa Opera and Ballet Theatre is considered one of the greatest cultural monuments. Once here were performing Tchaikovsky, Chaliapin and Sobinov. Attending this theater is a dream of theater connoisseur. The most unusual house of Odessa can be found in the Vorontsov Street. This is a building of a triangular shape, which seems to be absolutely flat from some angles. This is a truly unique architectural project, and so you will never find a building like this one anywhere in the world.

An interesting symbol of the city is the Potemkin Stairs. According to historical data, it appeared in this place long before Odessa was founded. The steps lead to the top of a hill on which a Turkish fortress once stood. The Potemkin Stairs have been preserved almost completely; during the last reconstruction in 1933, it lost only 8 of their steps. The whole stairway was asphalted, and beautiful pink granite was used for its finishing. Today on the top of the hill there is a beautiful park where you can walk among the trees, admire some interesting monuments and appreciate the city's panorama.

Another outstanding architectural monument is the Neo-Gothic Shah's Palace. This magnificent building got such a name due to the fact that the Persian Shah Mohammad Ali Shah Qajar had spent several days here. He was forced to flee to Odessa during the revolution in Iran. The beautiful palace built in the middle of the 19th century originally belonged to a Polish aristocrat; today the historic building is privately owned.

A beautiful historic building houses Odessa Museum of Western and Oriental art that opened back in the year 1923. The museum's exposition is considered to be one of the largest in the country. Its walls keep a unique collection of works by European and Asian artists and sculptors, as well as many works of art dating back to ancient times.

Odessa also has a very interesting archaeological museum that was founded a long time ago, in 1825. Currently, the museum halls present unique exhibits that discovered in various parts of the world. A large part of the exposition is devoted to the history of Ancient Egypt, as well as of ancient Rome and Greece. Many people come to this museum just to admire ancient jewelry made of precious metals.

The city's most unusual architectural monument can be called Odessa Passage built back in the 19th century. Today, the beautiful historic building with a glass roof houses a prestigious hotel and several boutiques. In the pre-revolutionary period, it housed the city's most prestigious shops. The main feature of the building is a locomotive adorning its roof.

Culture: sights to visit

Culture of Odessa. Places to visit old town, temples, theaters, museums and palaces

Each street of the city of Odessa features plenty of landmarks and monuments of historic significance. It is rather hard to distinguish the most important sights and landmarks among them. However a few objects deserve special attention of guests and tourists. Among religious landmarks of Odessa the Church of the Dormition which was built in the 19th century and was badly damaged during the war is of great tourist interest. The building of the church was restored only in the middle of the 20th century. Today the church is a significant pilgrimage of orthodox Christians. The church keeps ancient icons and other relics.

Another spot of tourist interest in Odessa is the Cathedral. The first religious building on the place of the Cathedral was erected as far back as in 1841. But in a few years the first church was totally ruined and a construction of the scale cathedral was started. The height of the cathedral with a bell tower is 56m.

The most attractive and favorable place for hiking in Odessa is still Deribasovskaya Street. It hosts several significant samples of architecture and known statuary groups. The street will lead to the City Garden (Gorodskoy Sad). The garden is an age mate of the city. It stuns the tourists and city residents with its majesty and beauty. The same attractive and astonishing destination in Odessa is the Pushkinskaya Street which has inherited its name from the famous author Alexander Pushkin. This is exactly the place where the famous author and poet lived. Today in a legendary house number 13 a museum (Alexander Pushkin Museum) dedicated to the creative work and life of the poet is located.

A brand identity of the city of Odessa is Pymorsky Boulevard which will be of great interest for hiking and touring enthusiasts. The boulevard hosts an ancient building of stock exchange, Alexander Pushkin monument and several memorials dedicated to military machines. This is exactly a place of location of a significant sample of architecture which is the Vorontsov Palace. The palace was built in 1826.

Odessa offers its guests several dozens of museums for exploration. Each of the museums offers unique collections of showpieces. One of the most visited museums is the Odessa Archeological Museum, the Wax Museum is a perfect destination for a family visit. Pictorial art admirers will love the Museum of Western and Eastern Art and those tourists wishing to get a deeper insight into the history of the city will find interesting the Local History Museum. Another interesting cultural destination is the Museum of Partisan Glory which is located in the underground tunnels of the war period.

Attractions & nightlife
City break in Odessa. Active leisure ideas for Odessa attractions, recreation and nightlife

Odessa is a popular tourist destination in Ukraine which offers its guests various entertainments fitting each taste and budget. Open air leisure enthusiasts should necessarily visit the City Garden (Gorodskoy Sad). In the heart of the Garden guests will find great music fountain surrounded with benches and arbors. The garden will be a perfect place for hiking. This is a place of location of several popular restaurants.

The Odessa Zoo is a next must visit place in the city. The exploration of the nature reserve will be of great interest and pleasure as for adults so for the youngest visitors. Among its inhabitants the guests will find many species of exotic animals brought there from far countries. The zoological park has recently been reconstructed. It has got new modernized specious enclosures for animals. To hunt some memorable gifts as well as fresh foods tourists should set to one of the local markets.

The largest food market in Odessa is the famous Privoz offering its visitors the vastest choice of vegetables, fruits as well as fresh sea foods. Fresh shrimps and fish are delivered there right from the port area of the city. The visitors of the market will be stunned with low prices. Another attractive market is set in the park near the Cathedral square. The main goods offered there are souvenirs and art objects.

One will find there beautiful paintings, buy original decorations and finery and crafts made of sea shells as well as other crafts of local masters. Another interesting market to visit in Odessa is the Starokonny one. A few centuries ago the best horses in Odessa were sold there. Today the market offers various pets from common parrots and dogs to exotic spiders and snakes. Many people visit the market as a zoological park as in a variety of performed animals the market equals to a zoo.

In search of shopping entertainments in large stores tourists may visit such shopping and entertaining centers as Metro and Europa. Among hundreds of stores and boutiques located in the centers one will find tons of brand clothes and footwear fitting every taste and fancy. Tourists should also pay attention to a large choice of night clubs and bars being of great popularity among local youth and city guests. The Exit club will be of great interest for extreme party fans and unique atmosphere admirers. Blues fans are recommended to visit the Wild Z bar (Diky Z) which is located in the basement of one of the historical buildings not far from the city center.

Cuisine & restaurants

Cuisine of Odessa for gourmets. Places for dinner best restaurants
Odessa meets its guests with numerous gastronomy establishments of different trends. Tourists will find small cozy cafés for sweets addicts, numerous pizza houses for genuine Italian treat fans, several exotic eating houses for genuine gourmands and traditional restaurants for those travelers interested in ethnic cuisine. Among the most in

demand restaurants of Odessa the Olio Pizza house is best worth attention of the city guests. The eating house offers genuine Italian pizza baked in a real oven. The house speciality is a real culinary masterpiece. Visitors can complement their meal with a speciality cocktail or a glass of astonishing wine.

The Golden Fleece ("Zolotoe Runo") restaurant specializes in traditional European cuisine. Its visitors can set comfortable in soft cozy arm chairs. The hall of the restaurant is decorated in warm cream tones and shades. The menu of the eating house presents popular Ukrainian dishes. The guests will discover an excellent choice of treats of Italian and Spanish cuisine as well. One of the main features of the eating house is an impressive sizing of served treats.

The most attractive city café is the Je To café. Its interior is executed in the inimitable style of the 17th century. The hall of the café is filled with romantic cozy atmosphere, the guests are offered to try and taste speciality desserts and aroma coffee. In the evening the café is filled with music and regular visitors. That is why a table for dinner should be reserved in advance. Sweets addicts will love another cozy café named Confectionary ("Tsukernya").

The café is as well decorated in the impressive style of foregone centuries. Its hall features antique furniture, paintings and live flowers. However visitors are attracted not only with the design of the interior but with a huge shining show window presenting a vast choice of delicious mouth wetting cakes and pies. To complement dainty sweet treats the visitors may order a cup of Brazilian aroma coffee or speciality fruit tea. The city center hosts a popular restaurant named "Basilik" which is a perfect location for a family visit greeting the guests with a vast choice of dainty treats.

The menu of the restaurant offers excellent meat treats, sea foods delicacies as well as a huge selection of salads and desserts. Affordable pricing is one of the major advantages of the eating house. A legendary gastronomy destination of the city and its genuine landmark is a beer restaurant "Gambrinus". It has been serving city residents and its guests since 1883. Then the main visitors of the pub were mostly boatmen and dock workers. Though since that time many features of the restaurant have drastically changed, still the highest quality beer and exciting speciality treats are still there on the menu. The restaurant features a unique original interior design. Instead of tables the hall of the restaurant is equipped with huge oak casks and instead of chairs the guests of the restaurant are offered small barrels.

Traditions & lifestyle

Colors of Odessa traditions, festivals, mentality and lifestyle
Cultural life in Odessa is rich in original holidays and exciting festivals. Many of the events are of global significance and attract a heavy traffic of foreign tourists. One of such events is a festival called Days of Europe which is held annually and falls on the third week of May. An

essential feature of the scale holiday is a variety of events taking place within the festival: children drawing contest, different exhibitions of photographic art, conferences, street concerts, kids' fests and culinary performances.

Gastronomy part of the festival deserves special attention of tourists. The Prymorsky Boulevard is a favorite destination of gastronomy tourism enthusiasts during the festival as this is exactly the place of holding numerous culinary shows, master classes and fairs dedicated to ethic cuisine.

The same interesting national holiday is the Independence Day which is celebrated on the 24th of August. In the morning hours the residents of the city come to the Kulikovo field where a grand military parade and military machines display take place. After the show a part of military machines are exhibited on the square and the exhibition lasts till the late evening. One of the most remarkable and exciting events of the holiday is a fair, where one can explore and buy different handicrafts of local masters.

The holiday of the Independence Day ends with a bright pyrotechnic show which takes place in the Victory Park. A city day is another scale holiday which falls on the 2nd of September. The festive day starts with a flower march taking place in the Prymorsky Boulevard. Unique compositions of unusual shapes are made of flowers specially for the fest. In the afternoon the Parade of Artists takes place in the

Deribasovskaya Street. Famous actors, artists and thespians take part in the march.

Several significant events take place on the square in front of the Vorontsov Palace. One of the events is a live chess play. The square is turned into a huge checkerboard and kids are engaged as chess pieces. Grand chess masters of international level are competing in chess playing art. It should be noted that a live chess play is one of the oldest and most exciting traditions of the holiday as it has been accompanying it for the last 200 years.

The holiday will be as well of great interest for music fans as the city day in Odessa is accompanied with various music events including as classic music concerts so grand rock festivals. Considering music traditions and events tourists should necessarily visit the Odessa jazz carnival which is held in the end of September. Famous music bands and amateur musicians are engaged in the carnival.

Tips for tourists

Preparing your trip to Odessa: advices & hints things to do and to obey
1. Odessa features a wide network of public transport including buses, trams and trolleybuses. A cost of a bus trip will totally depend of the length of a trip meanwhile a cost of a trip in trams and trolleybuses is fixed. Fare should be paid to a busman in a passenger compartment. A popular city transport means is a route taxi bus which stops only on

demand. These taxi buses should be stopped with a hand rise. However the buses can be stopped in such a way only from bus stops.

2. The Tandem bicycle rental center is in demand among those tourists giving preference to active leisure. Apart from two wheel transport the center provides skate boards and rollers.

3. Tourists visiting Odessa for the first time should first set to one of the tourist information offices. One of the best centers is located in the Pushkinskaya Street. The center offers its visitors free city maps and leaflets with descriptions of landmarks and monuments. The assistants of the office will inform the tourists on upcoming cultural events and will help to organize the leisure and touring program of the vacation.

4. Only central streets of the city are safe and sound for night tours meanwhile the remote areas of the city should be explored only in the daytime and only with a guide. Setting off to the city exploration one should not keep valuables by oneself without any need.

5. In public places one should be cautious and beware of pickpockets who are the main problem of the city. Railway stations, airport, in restaurants and shopping centers are those places to keep an eye on begs and overcoats.

6. The best place to hunt some memorable gifts and souvenirs is one of the local markets as these offer a vast choice of goods at prices

which are considerably lower than these in large stores. Bargaining is a must at the markets as this helps to reduce a price for desired goods by 10 15%.

7. The optimum way to pay for goods and services is national currency though large stores and restaurants accept US dollars and Euro apart from national hrivna. Currency can be exchanged in one of the local banks or in private exchange offices which are located on the premises of the airport and railway station.

8. Tourists looking for cruising the city by taxi should better call a taxi car by phone. One can take a car in the street as there are numerous "individual" drivers cruising the city. These are recommended only for big companies of travelers. At night one should use only official city taxi services.

Saky

Guide to Saky

Sightseeing in Saky what to see. Complete travel guide
Saki is often called the "city that extends life". It is famous for its unique balneological centers and there are no similar centers in other countries. Modern travelers have a wide choice of recreation houses, wellness centers and health camps for any taste and budget. Enchanting wild beaches, the amazingly clean and warm Black Sea, a

variety of landscapes, and a welcoming atmosphere of the old resort town attract many tourists.

Most of the tourists are those who want to undergo recovery procedures in one of the modern centers but the town is also popular with fans of beach recreation. Saki is distinguished by a peaceful atmosphere and a relaxed lifestyle. There are almost no noisy entertainment venues and crowded streets. However, the choice of enchanting beaches, beautiful places for walks and comfortable restaurants is really huge here.

The first mud baths were opened in 1827. Today, travelers can choose from dozens of holiday and special recreation houses. The main value of the resort is unique muds, the deposits of which are located right along the coastline. Many wellness resorts are very different from those attracting more tourists. The resort guests have a unique opportunity to relax at the wonderful beach and undergo enchanting beaches at the same time, as healing mud is literally under their feet.

Besides invaluable mud deposits on the territory of the resort, there are healing mineral springs and salt Saki Lake. It should be noted that the lake is a true local attraction associated with a lot of ancient legends. Besides upscale recreation houses and wellness centers, the resort is famous for its attractions, the most famous of which is the Resort Park.

The town will definitely impress those who love combining peaceful beach recreation with leisurely strolls along picturesque places and tourists with children. From year to year, the infrastructure is only developing and the guests of the resort have more prospects for an unforgettable vacation.

Fans of exciting excursions should definitely visit the Kara-Tobe Museum located on top of the namesake hill. This hill has a great value from an archeological point of view. The ruins of the Greek and Scythian settlements were found on its top. Today, the museum houses archeological exhibits found here. It is located in the historic building that belonged to the Black Sea Fleet. Today, there is an excellent viewing platform on the roof of the historic building.

The most beautiful religious monument is the Cathedral of St. Elijah located on Revolution Square. This cathedral was built at the beginning of the 20th century. It is one of the few religious constructions in the region that were not destroyed after the Revolution. It has been recently reconstructed, so tourists can view it in all its glory now.

In the surroundings of the resort, there is the ostrich farm called Sergiyev Posad. Tours to this farm are very popular with tourists with children. Besides ostriches, you can see here pheasants and quails. There is a big cage with deer. The entire territory of the complex is open for visitors. They have an opportunity to care for animals themselves and see the friendliest dwellers.

Besides famous Sassanian Lake, one of the main nature attractions of the resort is salt lake Sasyk-Sivash. The water here is beautiful pink because of rare minerals and crystal salt deposits. For many years, healing salt and mud had been produced from the lake. At one time, they were really expensive.

In the Saskian district, there is the biggest waterpark on the Crimean peninsula. It is called "Banana Republic". It was opened in 2005. 2 000 people can relax on the territory of the water park at the same time. It offers its visitors 8 beautiful pools, including special children's ones. The visitors can choose from 20 water rides that will impress the smallest children, as well as fans of extreme. There is the vast recreation area with loungers and bungalows. There are also a lot of restaurants and cafes in the water park.

Sevastopol

Guide to Sevastopol
Sightseeing in Sevastopol what to see. Complete travel guide
The hero city with a rich history started welcoming tourists a few years ago. Sevastopol was founded as the main base of the Russian fleet in 1783. The city has managed to maintain such an important status to this day. In addition, Sevastopol is an attractive tourist center today.

The city attracts many travelers with plenty of attractions and incredibly beautiful beaches.

On the territory of Sevastopol, there are a lot of preserved architectural monuments, some of which are aged over 200 years. Here, you can see fascinating mansions built in the 18th-19th centuries, walk along lovely winding streets, and admire the beauty of the nature. The city was significantly damaged in the period of the Great Patriotic War. The biggest part of its invaluable historical heritage was irrevocably lost. Due to the locals' effort, the city was quickly restored after the war. The citizens still remember about the great deeds of the defenders of Sevastopol.

Sevastopol has long been the most visited resort city of Crimea. Each year, about 10 million people vacation here. From year to year, the tourist infrastructure of the modern city is being improved. There are all the conditions for interesting pastime and comfortable recreation of the guests of Sevastopol. Most of the tourists are fans of beach recreation. Besides, Sevastopol is very popular with fans of excursion tourism.

In the city and its immediate surroundings, there are hundreds of interesting places to explore. There are not only historic constructions and museums, but also unique nature attractions. There are over 2 000 monuments dedicated to military and labor deeds of the locals.

Sevastopol is located in the south-western part of the Crimean peninsula. One of the main distinctive features of this land is plenty of wonderful secluded bays. There are over 30 bays along the coastline. Such an amazing choice of leisure areas will definitely impress those travelers who prefer to spend their time in secluded places. The city is also not without noisy entertainment venues. There are excellent leisure centers for the whole family, lively disco and night clubs, sports centers, and a lot of attractive gastronomic places.

In the immediate surroundings of Sevastopol, there are several important archeological districts. Those who like walking along historical places have an opportunity to visit the ruins of the old city called Chersonesus Taurica. Some researches suppose that this old Greek town was founded in the 5th century BC and had existed for over 1.5 thousand years. Consequently, the city was completely destroyed by nomadic tribes. Its ruins were found only in the 19th century. Now, most of the old constructions are restored in the archeological area.

The interesting monument in antique style is the Tower of the Winds built in the 19th century. Originally, the tower was built for the local library but it was destroyed in a large fire in 1955. The tower decorated with interesting bas-reliefs has been survived to this day and now is one of the main values of the city.

The beautiful historic building of the late 19th century is occupied by the Sevastopol Art Museum. It houses the unique collection of sculptures, paintings, and drawings of world-famous masters. Here, you can see works of great masters of Flemish Painting School and of famous Renaissance artists. The museum presents the exhibits of different periods. Some of them are aged over 300 years.

The unique religious monument here is Inkerman Cave Monastery located in the immediate surroundings of the city. The exact date of its construction is unknown. The first written references to it date back to the 8th century. In the middle of the 19th century, the monastery fell into decline and was reconstructed not so long ago. The historic building has been recently reconstructed but it is located in the picturesque natural area.

In the territory of the city, there is the Cathedral of Protecting Veil of the Mother of God that is the most religious construction in Sevastopol. It was built in the 19th-20th century but was closed after the Revolution in 1917. It gained its religious status back in the period of the Great Patriotic War. At that time, the building was partially destroyed. It started to be reconstructed in 1947 and then served as a gym. Masses were resumed here only in 1994.

Simeiz

Guide to Simeiz

Sightseeing in Simeiz what to see. Complete travel guide
The enchanting Crimean town Simeiz is a popular holiday destination. This picturesque resort village is very different from many big tourist centers. There are a lot of wonderful beaches and the nature is beautiful here. However, there is absolutely no noise and bustle that are typical for big resorts. The irreplaceable symbols of the resort and its main attractions are unusual mountains and rocks, which names speak for themselves: the Cat, the Maiden and the Panea.

The amazing garden town is literally drown in green plantings. Simeiz is perfectly suitable not only for beach recreation, but also for hiking. All the town streets are decorated with very interesting landscape attractions. Sightseeing tours are some of the main travelers' entertainments. Evergreen parks, magnificent mountains, natural beaches without complex constructions... The appearance of the resort is really natural, which is its main value.

As for the incredible nature, the favorable climate at the resort should be noted. To improve your health, it is not necessary to visit wellness centers here. It is enough to spend more time by the sea and in the open air. The atmosphere of the resort has a positive effect on the body. For those who want to undergo a set of recovery procedures should choose one of the excellent health centers.

Simeiz offers not only wonderful nature and upscale wellness centers, but also rich cultural heritage, the acquaintance with which will certainly diverse your recreation. Most of the excursion objects are unique nature attractions but fans of walking along historical places will not be bored too. Several interesting attractions are located in the territory of the resort town. In the surroundings of Simeiz, there are the most extraordinary and most interesting historical monuments.

Walking along the town, fans of sightseeing tours can get lots of positive emotions too. Literally, at each step, you can see beautiful sculptures and luxurious villas that look really inimitable in the midst of the wonderful nature. Simeiz is a perfect recreation place for those who want to vacation in a harmonious atmosphere and see the beauty of the Crimean nature.

At the resort, there are a lot of preserved beautiful old villas that are now considered as main architectural monuments. One of the most beautiful villas is called Ksenya built at the beginning of the 20th century. The first owner of the luxurious villa in the modern style was Countess V. A. Tchuykevitch. The building is distinguished by the diversity of terraces and loggias. Today, this historic building is in private ownership, so no excursions are organized here. The resort guests will have an opportunity to admire its exterior. When walking through the historical district, you can see other beautiful villas built over a hundred years ago.

Fans of water entertainments should visit the waterpark called the Blue Bay. This waterpark is one of the largest and most popular on the

Crimean peninsula. In its territory, there are well-equipped recreation areas for adults and children of different age. There are special children's pools, rides for the littlest visitors, a climbing wall, and different playgrounds. In the waterpark, there are several comfortable cafes, so you can spend the whole day here.

As for the religious monuments of the resort, the Cathedral of St. Blessed Virgin is worth being mentioned. It was finished not so long ago, in 2008. The church was built according to the beautiful historical traditions, so it is distinguished by a spectacular exterior. The church is located on the hilltop and surrounded by lush plants. The excursion will definitely impress fans of hiking along picturesque places.

The perfect place for strolling and admiring nature is the Central Simeiza Park. Here, you can see luxurious palms, pines, and cypresses. It also has another unique feature: There is one of the largest juniper groves in the region. The pastime here is considered as an effective treatment procedure. The main park of the resort is well-equipped. There are comfortable walking paths, pavilions, and benches.

Another interesting place is the Cypress Alley, which is a spectacular avenue decorated with rows of thin cypresses. This alley has a wonderful view of the mountains. Besides plants and flowers, it is also decorated with multiple sculptures. That is why the prospect is officially called the Alley of Apollos.

Simferopol

Guide to Simferopol

Sightseeing in Simferopol what to see. Complete travel guide
Simferopol is one of the largest cities in the Autonomous Republic of Crimea in Ukraine. The city is located between the Inner and Outer chains of the Crimean Mountains in the valley Salgir River. Simferopol is a really important economic, administrative and cultural center of Ukraine.

The capital of Crimea is full of interesting historical sights and monuments. The city has monuments devoted to Prince Dolgorukiy, Suvorov, famous people of culture and art, heroes of World War II, and the memorial to the victims of Stalin's expulsions of 1944. In front of the Supreme Soviet of the Autonomous Republic of Crimea you will see the Soviet tank T-34 installed on the pedestal. The tank is set in honor of the city's liberation from Nazi occupation. Prince Mikhail Semenovich Vorontsov Palace is a well-known architectural monument. This palace is located in the Botanical Garden of the Taurida National University.

This city is also famous for its beautiful parks - Vorontsovsky Park, in which you will see a wonderful sight of landscape architecture the mansion of Pallas and the house of Count Vorontsov, and the urban recreation park with its wonderful atmosphere. Simferopol is famous for numerous cultural institutions located in this city. The city's suburbs are no less interesting as here you will find Kebir Jami Mosque, the ruins of the ancient Scythian Naples city, a natural landmark named Snake Cave, Skelsky stalactite cave, the two-story mansion of Dinzer, and Republican Crimean Tatar Museum of Art.

Simferopol Kenasa is an interesting religious sight. It was built in the 19th century on the initiative of the local Karaim community. This construction is an amazing architectural monument, which combines elements of Moorish, Byzantine and Gothic style. At the beginning of the 20th century, the Kenasa came to desolation. Only in 2014, it became possible to complete its reconstruction and return the religious monument to the community.

No less interesting sight of the 19th century is the Holy Trinity Cathedral. Several years ago, a convent was founded in the area. The temple was built in the best tradition of classical style. Sky-blue domes, unique Corinthian capitals, and arches are its distinctive features. This temple is one of the few in the region that continued to function even in Soviet times. It's a miracle it managed to avoid destruction so typical for those times. Currently, visitors can admire the most beautiful elements of old design. Many unique religious artifacts are kept in the walls of the church.

Gorgeous Alexander Nevsky Cathedral was founded in 1829. However, the construction that the guests of Simferopol see now, has been erected only recently. In 1930, they blew a beautiful cathedral up, as hundreds of other religious buildings. The revival of the ancient church began in 1999. Modern architects managed to erect a cathedral for 4 years. They created a beautiful garden, paths for walks, and equipped recreation areas.

Central Museum of Tauris occupies one of the most beautiful historic buildings nowadays. It presents diverse and exciting expositions. The museum has collections of unique ethnographic pieces and archaeological finds, discovered in the immediate vicinity of Simferopol. There is also an extensive natural-science exposition. Medieval jewelry and engravings are considered one of the most valuable exhibits.

Among specialized museums, the Museum of Chocolate is worth noting. As one can guess by name, all its pieces are made of chocolate. The museum has a small cafe, where you can taste brand cakes and pastries. Those with a sweet tooth can visit an excellent candy store.

Culture: sights to visit

Culture of Simferopol. Places to visit old town, temples, theaters, museums and palaces
Simferopol is sure to appeal to fans of exciting excursions, as there are many interesting sights in the city. The Vorontsov Palace is located in a beautiful park; it is a prominent landmark in the classical style. The palace was built in 1826for the governor Naryshkin; there he hosted a

lot of famous guests. Next to the palace there is the old botanical garden, which is also one of the city's attractions.

To get acquainted with the city's history and cultural traditions of local people visit the Crimean Ethnographic Museum. It was founded in 1923, but with the outbreak of the Second World War it has ceased to exist and was re-opened relatively recently, in 1992. The museum's exhibition includes more than 4 thousand exhibits, most of which were donated by local residents.

Scythian Naples, the ruins of ancient Scythian capital, is another interesting attraction. Archaeologists have restored the center of the old town located at the top of the hill. Guests of this unique open-air museum can stroll through the historic main square and admire the spectacular building with columns - the mausoleum - where remains of Scythian nobility are stored.

One of the most beautiful buildings of the city is the Kebir-Jami Mosque. It was founded in 1508 and is the oldest object in the city. The mosque is open to all comers; tourists would definitely appreciate fine interior design of the shrine. There are interesting natural attractions in Simferopol, one of which is located near the downtown.

The chestnut tree with five trunks was planted in 1829; according to one of the versions, five chestnut kernels were dropped into one hole, and that led to the unusual appearance of the tree. Currently height of chestnut is about 25 meters and diameter is about 5 meters. Locals care about the tree, so every year it becomes more solid and impressive. There are also quite unusual excursion objects in Simferopol, such as the Chocolate Museum. Among its exhibits are true works of art, including models of world-famous attractions, portraits of prominent men of art and unusual artistic compositions. As you can guess by the name, all the exhibits are made of chocolate.

The Salt Lake Tabernacle is a famous attraction of historical importance in the capital of Utah. It was erected in 1867 to host Mormon meetings (the official name of the religious denomination sounds like "The Church of Jesus Christ of Latter-day Saints"). At the time when the tabernacle was built, the construction was so striking in its architecture that it ranked among the wonders of the world. Frank Lloyd Wright also noted the high architectural value of the building and even called it "one of the architectural masterpieces of the country or, possibly, of the whole world". Many tourists will agree with him after seeing the tabernacle even from a distance. It is no less astonishing on the inside. A magnificent organ one of the largest in the entire world is situated inside this building and brought it fame. Besides, the musical instrument earned the praise of many well-known personalities. Among them, you can find Jack Betards, the President of Schoenstein & Co (the oldest and largest organ builder in the western United States).

One more point of interest in Salt Lake City that is worthy of mentioning is the unparalleled Cathedral of the Madeleine. The construction of the place of worship was completed in 1909. In its architecture, elements of neo-Gothic and Neo-Romanesque style can be recognized. It is interesting to note that the facade of the building is decorated with images of saints. On the eastern wall, you can see an image of Joan of Arc, meanwhile, images of John the Baptist and Vincent de Paul can be observed on the western wall. Characters of the Old Testament and the magnificent gargoyles are also represented here and will amaze any tourist. We would like to point out that the cathedral inspired the famous American writer Dan Brown to write his outstanding work "The Da Vinci Code". This is the reason the shrine is valued as a cinematic and literary landmark.

You should not overlook the beautiful Joseph Smith Memorial Building, where there are several rooms that give you an opportunity to plunge deeper into the local culture. There is, for instance, a historic room with a preserved interior of the end of the 19th century. In this room, you will also come across a large white statue of Joseph Smith, the founder of the Mormon Church. There are also some places for your entertainment. Interesting productions, for example, are often staged at the Heritage Theater. If you are looking for a great view, then from the windows of restaurants "The Roof" and "The Garden" you can behold a stunning panorama of the city. In addition, thematic events are often held in the halls of the building, thus attracting people interested in enriching themselves culturally. Initially, there was a hotel situated here, which once received only representatives of the white race (and this rule also applied to well-known personalities). The hotel was built in 1911 in the neo-renaissance style, but in 1987 it ceased its activities in this capacity.

One of the few well-preserved estates called Wheeler Historic Farm deserves tourist's attention. It is a Victorian manor of the end of the 19th century with the interior related to that time. The complex includes agricultural and handicraft buildings, as well as residential buildings. It is framed by an impressive garden with ponds and paths, where you should definitely take a walk. Another notable historic building is the residence of the first governor of Utah, Brigham Young. We are talking about the Beehive House, which was built in 1854. The construction got the name "bee house" due to the well visible statue of the hive (which symbolizes hard work) that is at the very top of the roof. The house is rather large, and the reason for this is legendary. The fact is that, like many Mormons, the first governor was a polygamist.

The government buildings of Salt Lake City are also worth seeing and visiting. These include The Governor's Mansion the residence of the current governor of Utah. The magnificent building was built in 1902 and back then served as the center of the cultural life of local bohemians. It was the venue for theatrical and orchestral performances, as well as balls and dances. Many famous political and religious figures also visited it, for example, President Theodore Roosevelt was among them. The building became the residence of the governor in 1937 but did not fulfill this function in the period from 1957 to 1977. A library and a museum were located here during these years. The Salt Lake Masonic Temple is also worth mentioning. It was built in 1920 and was decorated with Masonic symbols, both inside and outside. The building itself is an excellent example of the Egyptian Renaissance.

Built in 1900, the Alfred McCune Mansion is another remarkable building in the capital of Utah. It catches the eye immediately with its stunning architecture. The original owner of the house wanted only one thing: that his house should be so extravagant and unusual that it would immediately speak of his bright personality. He therefore hired the architect, C. C. Dallas, who created for him a masterpiece of eclecticism, mixing elements of Gothic revival with the style of East Asia. Thanks to this decision, today travelers can see the magnificent building and admire it. After 1920, when the first owners left the house, the building was turned into a music school and served this purpose until 1957. Brigham Young University was situated here during the 16 years that followed (1957-1973). Nowadays, from 1997, a cultural center is located here.

The Great Salt Lake, which gave the city its name, is another significant place that you should not miss. It is especially popular among fans of eco-tourism. In addition to the lake, you can find other beautiful natural attractions in and around the city. The Big Cottonwood Canyon, for example, is among them. It is one of the best places for climbing, cycling, setting up a picnic, or fishing. It should be noted that the trail leading to the canyon is no less picturesque when compared with the natural landmark itself. Parks located in the center of the city are great spaces to achieve pacification. We are referring to the likes of Red Butte Garden, Liberty Park, and Gilgal Gardens, that are the most well-liked among citizens of Utah. Each of the green areas is more than worthy of a walk along.

Many tourists use the famous Pony Express National Historic Trail, which passes through five states (California, Colorado, Nevada, Utah, and Wyoming), to explore the local culture. You can do it yourself by vehicles, bicycles or on horseback the options are unlimited. The route represents the way which the horsemen used while delivering mail between 1860 and 1861. The system was so debugged that it was famous outside the country. There are several cultural venues that would give travelers wonderful impressions at theatrical shows and concerts of classical music. The Capitol Theater, the Eccles Theater, as well as the Utah Symphony concert hall are great examples of such places. In addition, plenty of interesting themed events and festivals are held in the Gallivan Center.

Museums are great for exploring the local history and culture, as well as having a great time. You can get acquainted with the story of how the city was founded in the cultural center of the Pioneer Memorial Museum. This place is the best option for those who want to learn something that cannot be read in history textbooks. The Leonardo Museum, dedicated to the Italian genius, is fascinating with its exhibits. The organizers tried to recreate outstanding projects of an eminent inventor and artist. The cultural sight acquaints visitors with science and the laws of the world as a whole. Locals are so fond of the Toyota Land Cruiser that they even dedicated a separate museum to it the Land Cruiser Heritage Museum. There you can find such a huge number of cars of this kind, that the collection will impress even the most sophisticated tourist.

The Fort Douglas Military Museum is a great place to explore the history of the US Civil War. The museum occupies the territory of the fort, which was built in 1862 and played an important role at this time. If in the company of kids, you should go to the cultural center, Discovery Gateway Children's Museum. Your children can learn a lot of educational information about the world around them, right here. Another remarkable museum in Salt Lake City is the Chase Home Museum of Utah Folk Art, which presents works of art created by local artists. There are many beautiful sculptures in the capital of Utah, among which statues like National Pony Express Monument and Mormon Battalion Monument stand out in a special way. The picturesque Brigham Young Historic Park is also famous for its magnificent sculptural compositions.

Attractions & nightlife

City break in Simferopol. Active leisure ideas for Simferopol attractions, recreation and nightlife

Simferopol is a popular family resort that has all the best for an exciting and varied pastime. Travelers who like to relax outdoors should definitely visit local parks; the most famous among them is the Salgirka park. Here you can relax with your family, have a picnic or just walk around extensive grounds of the park. The Pioneer bowling center would be a perfect place for a family holiday.

Fans of this sport will appreciate excellent facilities of the club; beginners could take a couple of lessons from a professional coach. It is worth noting that the bowling center has an excellent restaurant. Fans of billiards like the trendy Tsarskaya Ohota bar. Here you can enjoy your favorite game in a relaxed atmosphere and have a pair of signature cocktails in the bar, where there is always a very nice friendly ambience.

There some suitable places for fans of night entertainment programs. One of the most popular nightclubs is KING. The stylish interior, great sound quality and carefully planned entertainment program made the club one of the most popular venues of the city. The title of the Cobra nightclub is fully consistent with its subject. Its design is laid out in detail; visitors are offered to stay on couches with upholstery that resembles the reptile skin. There is also a great bar at the front of which you can see the main character - a statue of Cobra.

The Globus club invites visitors to have fun and enjoy signature treats. Vibrant parties take place here few times a week. You should definitely include a visit to local shops to the entertainment program. Most popular souvenirs among tourists are Crimean wines. It's better to choose wines in Nastoyashie Vina Kryma shopping pavilion, as a range of products is very wide there.

Sports fans will enjoy Extreme Crimea shop, where one can buy stylish outfit of good quality. For jewelry it's worth go to the Ktaros store, where very interesting author articles of precious metals are sold. Simferopol is famous for an abundance of colorful markets; the most famous among them are San Marino, Sevastopol Market, Central Market and Balaclava Market.

One of the most cherished celebrations of the locals is Maslenitsa, a holiday whose roots go back to pagan times. Traditional pancakes with tea drinking, burning of an effigy symbolizing Judas, mass folk celebrations, and interactive contests, are all integral parts of the festival. Generally, the time of celebration of the festival falls on mid-

February (depending on the date of the beginning of Easter). During the festival, an interesting cultural program awaits the guests of the city: an art exhibition is held at the Museum of the City's History (Muzey Istorii Goroda Simferopolya), traditional celebrations with burning straw effigies, picnics, and interactive contests are organized in the Trenyov Square.

Clubbers will be happy to attend a festival dedicated to trance, and whose name speaks for itself. We are talking about the event Trancemission, which is marked at the beginning of May or the end of September. The venue of the event is usually the huge sports complex of the Crimean Federal University named after Vernadsky. Nevertheless, sometimes the complex Connect Center is used as the venue. It is a platform where you can dance until morning. Participants of the festival include famous DJs who try with all their might to please the visitors so that they will all receive only the most pleasant impressions. Not a single incendiary party can do without art installations and a laser show, which have long been the hallmark of the festival.

The capital of Crimea gladdens fans of cultural festivals. Subsequently, in the middle of April in the Scientific Library of Ivan Franko (in the National University of Lviv), a festival dedicated to the birthday of the outstanding poet Nikolay Gumilyov takes place, verses of whom many locals read out. Events dedicated to the author take place in other major cities of Crimea in Koktebel and Theodosia but those in Simferopol are the most large-scale. They include poetry reading and literary meetings with contemporary authors, as well as awarding winners the Nikolay Gumilyov Prize. Immediately after the poetic festival, a holiday dedicated to French culture starts. The venue of this holiday is the same Ivan Franko Scientific Library, where at this time you can see films about French culture, as well as be witness to musical concerts.

The end of October in Simferopol means that the Coffee and Tea Expo is approaching. In the exhibition complex Connect Center, not only can you taste delicious coffee, but you also get to watch barista competitions that have contestants coming from all over Crimea, as well as get high-quality master classes in the preparation of drinks and cupping. The fest is competitive in nature, being a qualifying round the best barista is later sent to the capital of Russia to represent Crimea. The festival also hosts an exhibition of confectionery "Tortida", which allows you to enjoy coffee and tea and have a snack. It is worth noting that this is one of the most popular events among local residents.

Another fascinating gastronomic festival is held in early February and is called "Gastroly". Exhibition complex "Connect Center" again receives guests who want to enjoy the wonderful culinary delights. In addition to the gastronomic program, which includes tasting dishes of local cuisine, cooking classes and the opening of food courts, visitors can expect animated shows, music concerts and specially equipped locations for engaging in sports. Special attention is paid to healthy food. Entrance, just like to most festivals of this kind (including the ones presented above), is free of charge.

Cuisine & restaurants

Cuisine of Simferopol for gourmets. Places for dinner best restaurants

Visit to Simferopol's restaurant will be a great addition to the rest, as in the city there are places suitable for everyone. Budget travelers like the Chisken House restaurant; its menu includes a lot of interesting dishes, desserts and soft drinks. Chisken House differs from the fast-food restaurants, which are familiar to most travelers; it serves great salads, fresh pastries, juices and fruit salads.

Gourmets and those who can't imagine a meal without gourmet fish dishes are advised to visit the Fish-Pab. Like any classic pub, it is ready to offer a huge selection of beers. One can spend a wonderful evening with friends in Fish-Pab. The 100 pudoff cafe is an amazing place; in addition to a large selection of treats, it offers visitors an interesting evening program. The cafe often hosts jazz evenings, bright fashion shows and presentations.

Those who wish to taste popular dishes of Ukrainian cuisine are recommended to look into the Anvis bar. All treats here are cooked following old recipes. The bar also features very colorful artwork. One of the most prestigious dining places of the city is the Matisse restaurant. It is perfect for banquets and special events. It is ready to offer a luxurious international menu and two banquet halls, one of which can accommodate more than 350 people.

Fans of Italian cuisine would appreciate the rich menu of the Parmezan restaurant. After tasting branded treats its visitors are offered hookah. The restaurant is a great place for a romantic dinner. One of the most popular places of the city is the Divan cafe; it specializes in cooking Tatar cuisine. The room of cafe is decorated in best traditions of the East; there is always a pleasant harmonious atmosphere here.

Among the budget places the City Cafe number 1 points out. Its menu includes a lot of attractive dishes; treats here are suitable for both vegetarians and meat lovers. All dishes have interesting decoration. One of the main advantages of the institutions remains competitive price policy. Among the gastronomic places of Simferopol pub with a romantic name - The Power of the Celt - points out. It will surprise visitors with an interesting decor and entertainment.

Traditions & lifestyle
Colors of Simferopol traditions, festivals, mentality and lifestyle
Simferopol is a typical modern resort with a continuously evolving infrastructure. The ancient city is rich in culture and tradition, acquaintance with which would give a lot of leisure experiences.

Travelers who visit the city during the second half of May will be able to participate in a very interesting national event - the Festival of Tatar culture. A significant part of Crimean population is represented by Tatars. At the 20th of May each year they gather in Simferopol to conduct a large-scale celebration.

The festival is always accompanied by massive public celebration; interesting concerts and competitions are held on streets of the city. Gastronomic events remain inescapable parts of the festival, where everyone can try national Tatar dishes and even learn how to cook them. Colorful fairs, where national Tatar costumes and decorations are sold, are sure to please fans of shopping. Youngest guests of the resort will enjoy an abundance of rides and attractions.

One of the city's main landmarks is a historic district; it is separated from the new district by the long street. Walking through these places will be an unforgettable experience, as this area is very amazing. On the one hand, narrow streets are full of beautiful modern buildings, well-maintained parks and landscaped courtyards, and on the other hand, there are old and dilapidated buildings there. Such a contrast of two times has turned the Old Town district to one of the city's main attractions. The modern city is constantly changing; locals are trying their best to keep its charm.

In the past few years an incredible amount of beautiful wooden figures has appeared on the city streets. Tourists are fond of searching and photographing them. The fact is that there are lots of old trees in Simferopol, many of which have been cut down. Local artists make works of art from those trunks and stumps of felled trees; they can be seen in various parts of the city. Beautiful and modern, Simferopol is a favorite holiday destination of thousands of tourists. This tranquil and picturesque city has interesting traditions and unique culture.

One of the most cherished celebrations of the locals is Maslenitsa, a holiday whose roots go back to pagan times. Traditional pancakes with tea drinking, burning of an effigy symbolizing Judas, mass folk celebrations, and interactive contests, are all integral parts of the festival. Generally, the time of celebration of the festival falls on mid-February (depending on the date of the beginning of Easter). During the festival, an interesting cultural program awaits the guests of the city: an art exhibition is held at the Museum of the City's History (Muzey Istorii Goroda Simferopolya), traditional celebrations with burning straw effigies, picnics, and interactive contests are organized in the Trenyov Square.

Clubbers will be happy to attend a festival dedicated to trance, and whose name speaks for itself. We are talking about the event Trancemission, which is marked at the beginning of May or the end of September. The venue of the event is usually the huge sports complex of the Crimean Federal University named after Vernadsky. Nevertheless, sometimes the complex Connect Center is used as the venue. It is a platform where you can dance until morning. Participants of the festival include famous DJs who try with all their might to please the visitors so that they will all receive only the most pleasant impressions. Not a single incendiary party can do without art installations and a laser show, which have long been the hallmark of the festival.

The capital of Crimea gladdens fans of cultural festivals. Subsequently, in the middle of April in the Scientific Library of Ivan Franko (in the National University of Lviv), a festival dedicated to the birthday of the outstanding poet Nikolay Gumilyov takes place, verses of whom many locals read out. Events dedicated to the author take place in other major cities of Crimea in Koktebel and Theodosia but those in Simferopol are the most large-scale. They include poetry reading and literary meetings with contemporary authors, as well as awarding winners the Nikolay Gumilyov Prize. Immediately after the poetic festival, a holiday dedicated to French culture starts. The venue of this holiday is the same Ivan Franko Scientific Library, where at this time you can see films about French culture, as well as be witness to musical concerts.

The end of October in Simferopol means that the Coffee and Tea Expo is approaching. In the exhibition complex Connect Center, not only can you taste delicious coffee, but you also get to watch barista competitions that have contestants coming from all over Crimea, as well as get high-quality master classes in the preparation of drinks and cupping. The fest is competitive in nature, being a qualifying round the best barista is later sent to the capital of Russia to represent Crimea. The festival also hosts an exhibition of confectionery "Tortida", which allows you to enjoy coffee and tea and have a snack. It is worth noting that this is one of the most popular events among local residents.

Another fascinating gastronomic festival is held in early February and is called "Gastroly". Exhibition complex "Connect Center" again receives guests who want to enjoy the wonderful culinary delights. In addition to the gastronomic program, which includes tasting dishes of local cuisine, cooking classes and the opening of food courts, visitors can expect animated shows, music concerts and specially equipped locations for engaging in sports. Special attention is paid to healthy food. Entrance, just like to most festivals of this kind (including the ones presented above), is free of charge.

Tips for tourists
Preparing your trip to Simferopol: advices & hints things to do and to obey
1. You can get to the city center from the airport by trolley bus route 9 or any of the numerous taxis. The city has excellent public transport system; buses and trolleybuses can literally get to any area of interest.

2. Day trips to nearby cities and resort areas are very popular among tourists; neighborhoods can be reached by train. A trip to Sevastopol

and Yevpatoria will take more than two hours and a journey to Bakhchisarai would take little more than half an hour.

3. In addition to public transport, taxi service is available for travelers at any time. The car can be called by phone or found on special parking spaces on the street; latest are usually close to major attractions and entertainment venues. Be sure to bargain with a taxi driver and negotiate the price before getting into the car.

4. In the city you can find a huge number of attractive restaurants, the prices in which will satisfy even the thriftiest travelers. Local shops also feature attractive prices for goods.

5. The high tourist season is from May to September, this time is the best for sightseeing and excursion trips. In summer it's better to book a hotel in advance, otherwise all affordable rooms can be occupied.

6. It is essential for holiday-makers to observe basic safety cautions. Don't use services of private individuals, as it is likely to become a victim of fraud. In no case your belongings should be left unattended; going for a walk, it's better to take just a small amount of cash.

7. You can safely walk along the central area of the city even late at night, as it is always very busy and noisy. The historic district of Simferopol isn't a best place to take stroll in the night; it would be better to explore it during the day accompanied by a tour group.

8. Those who like quiet and secluded places are recommended to plan a trip in late autumn or spring, when there aren't so many tourists in the city. In winter there is a very favorable weather, and many of the local hotels provide attractive discounts for their customers.

Sudak

Guide to Sudak

Sightseeing in Sudak what to see. Complete travel guide
Sudak is one of the most unusual Crimean resorts. It is just impossible to compare it with other resorts. Besides the magnificence typical for many Crimean resorts, it has a special atmosphere, thanks to which you can attune to comfortable and peaceful recreation for a few hours. Sudak has been a popular resort area for over a hundred years. Despite the huge number of tourists, Sudak has managed to preserve its pristine charm. In the city, there are almost no large residential and hotel complexes. There are also no big and noisy entertainment venues. Even local beaches where thousands of tourists relax every year have not lost their attractiveness.

Enchanting cottages crowned with grapes, winding streets with fragrant flowers, local merchants offering to buy house wine this is how modern travelers see Sudak. Those tourists who have got used to vacationing in comfortable conditions have a wide choice of boarding houses and hotels in Sudak. As a rule, all the wellness & recreation houses are located near the coast and have private beaches that are fully equipped for a wonderful pastime.

Sudak will definitely impress fans of sports entertainments who can diverse their leisure in different interesting ways in addition to visiting classic beach attractions. Hand-gliding, helicopter flight, romantic cruises and plenty of interesting places for walking and scuba diving... Sudak is not inferior to big Crimean resorts in entertainments. It is just impossible to imagine the holidays in Sudak without exploring picturesque surroundings. Travelers can choose among hundreds of interesting routes. Horse-riding is very popular with the guests of the resort. Hikers should not also worry about any obstacles.

Each year, Sudak is visited by 500 thousand people from all over the world. Their enthusiastic feedbacks are the best advertisement of the resort. Despite its small area and a lack of modern entertainment centers, Sudak is perfect for different kinds of sport. Harmonious beach recreation, sports tourism, health tourism, and the acquaintance with the historical past of the region no matter what kind of recreation you choose, positive emotions and memories are guaranteed.

Sudak is famous for its unique historical monuments and archeological districts. The spectacular monument of the Middle Ages is the Genoese Fortress built in the 14th-15th centuries. The fortress is located on top of the bluff rock that made the construction almost impregnable. Exactly this fact let the historical monument survive to this day. Now, the medieval fortress is a place where historical festivals and performances are regularly held. It is very interesting to visit the fortress in the context of the usual sightseeing tour. The top of the mountain has a spectacular view of the resort area.

The guests of Sudak can combine the sightseeing with active entertainments by visiting the big modern waterpark. Its square is over 2 hectares. On the territory of the waterpark, there are pools for children and adults and different rides. It is interesting to spend time in the waterpark even with small children, as there are special playgrounds for them. Extreme fans will not be bored here too, as there are several special rides.

The fans of sea entertainments should certainly drop in the local dolphinarium called "Nemo". Interesting performances with dolphins and sea lions are annually held for the visitors. A lot of additional services are also available for the guests of the dolphinarium. This also serves as a special wellness center. Here, children with different diseases can get the dolphin therapy. The visitors can swim with amazing sea dwellers in one pool and take interesting memorable pictures.

The beautiful historic building that served as the summer cottage of rich baron Funk before is occupied by the History Museum of Sudak now. It was opened in 1998 but the museum had not worked for a long time, as it was damaged significantly in a fire. It was reopened in 2004. Now, the rich collection of the museum is presented in 13 showrooms. Most of the exhibits are archeological artifacts that have been found in the surroundings of Sudak.

Ternopil

Guide to Ternopil

Sightseeing in Ternopil what to see. Complete travel guide
The picturesque city Ternopil is located on the Seret River and is one of the largest cities in Western Ukraine. It was founded as a fortress in the 16th century for protecting the Polish lands. The founder of the ancient city was hetman Jan Tarnowski who gave the name to the ancient city. The history of the city is rich with interesting events. At different times, it was under Russia, Austria and Poland, which had an impact on the formation of its cultural traditions.

One of the most important events in the history of Ternopil took place in 1672. The Turkish conquerors invaded the territory of the city and destroyed most of the buildings and fortifications. Then, Ternopil had long been abandoned. The city started to be restored only in the second half of the 18th century. Invaluable architectural monuments that you can admire today were built in the 18th-19th centuries. In the city, there are constructions created in different architectural styles.

The most spectacular architectural monuments are located in the center of the city that is almost pedestrian now. The walk through the center of Ternopil will become a real journey into the past, as picturesque streets have not almost changed for the last hundred years. One of the most beautiful and liveliest streets is Valovaya. Most of the tourists come here to see old architectural monuments.

Cultural traditions are very rich and interesting. Several amazing legends are associated only with the name of the city. According to one of them, it was named after its founder but many historians believe that the first settlements in the territory of the modern city appeared before the 16th century. As the legend says, the first settlers found here a big field. They improved the area overgrown with blackthorn and built here the beautiful city. Modern Ternopil is ready to offer its guests all the conditions for amazing recreation. The acquaintance with historical monuments and the natives' culture, romantic walks along the shore of the pond, relaxation at top-rated restaurants, plenty of shopping and entertainment centers the guests of Ternopil are not limited in choosing how to spend their leisure time.

In Ternopol, there are a lot of important religious monuments, including Dominican Church It was built in the middle of the 18th century and is a vivid example of the baroque style. The historical monument was seriously damaged during the war in 1944. After the Great Patriotic War, it started to be reconstructed. The building was restored completely only in 1957. The cathedral impresses with its delicate interior that was restored in accordance with historical traditions.

In the immediate surroundings of the city, there is St. Nicholas Church that was built at the initiative of the local Armenian diaspora in the middle of the 16th century. This church is a striking example of the Renaissance style. It had been constantly rebuilt and complemented with new architectural elements until the 18th century. When the Armenian community left this place in the middle of the 18th century, the church was in disrepair. In 1929, it laid almost in ruins. Then, it started to be restored. The church was rebuilt almost according to its original project. Nowadays, it is a historical monument of national significance.

Fans of hiking along historical places should visit the Terebovlyansk Castle that is also located in the surroundings of Ternopol. The castle was built for protecting the territory in the 10th century. For the first 300 years, it was repeatedly rebuilt and reconstructed. In the 14th century, the wooden castle was conquered by the Polish people who built it of stone. The historical construction has been partially preserved to this day. The adjacent area of the castle has a wonderful view of the neighborhood.

The beautiful architectural monument is the Palace of Prince Vyshnevetsky. It was built for the representatives of the eminent princely family in the 18th century. The big palace had been built for over 30 years. As the latest studies have shown, the palace started to be built on the foundation of the destroyed castle of the 14th century. In the period of the Great Patriotic War, the palace was partially destroyed but then was restored within a very short time. Now, it serves as the museum. Its collection includes interesting antique items, pieces of art, and the personal belongings of former owners.

Truskavets

Guide to Truskavets

Sightseeing in Truskavets what to see. Complete travel guide
The resort city Truskavets is located not far from Lviv. It started to attract travelers in the 19th century. In the territory of the city, there are healing mineral springs. There are upscale wellness centers around them. Every month, over 10 thousand tourists visit the resort. Most of them are guests from distant lands. The enchanting resort is famous not only for its top-rated wellness centers, but also with its unique nature. The environmental indicators of the city meet the highest standards. The resort is surrounded by vast woods on all sides.

Due to the amazing climate, the resort is perfectly suitable for family recreation. It is interesting to visit Truskavets not only in summer, but also in the cold season. Winters here are very gentle and snowy. Besides 14 springs of mineral water, there are deposits of healing minerals in Truskavets. Mineral wax, as well as salt "Barbara" that tourists often buy in specialized shops and bring to their homeland for recovery procedures, is produced here.

The wellness centers of Truskavets are ready to offer its clients a wide range of wellness programs. However, don't think that your vacation at this picturesque resort will limit itself to treatment procedures. Tourists have a worthy choice of places to walk. The acquaintance with the unique nature will bring you unforgettable emotions. From year to year, the infrastructure of the resort is developing. Today, you can find here a lot of attractive restaurants, pubs, disco and night clubs, most of which are located in the territory of the hotels.

Truskavets is ready to offer travelers quite an interesting excursion program. In the city, there are several interesting culture objects. It should be also noted that the resort is not expensive, so you can travel in a big company. Despite the fact that the peak of the tourist season is summer months, many travelers prefer to visit Truskavets on the New Year's Eve. The snow-covered city looks incredibly beautiful. At this time of the year, the main tourists' entertainment is skiing. In any season, the guests of Truskavets are welcomed and can expect their vacation to be interesting.

The guests of Truskavets can easily combine here traditional resort entertainments and interesting sightseeing tours. Fans of history will be impressed by St. Nicholas Church that was built in the second half of the 19th century. The first temple at its site was built at the beginning of the 16th century but then was destroyed completely. It was reconstructed for the first time almost 100 years ago. Its interior was renovated in the 90s of the last century. Today, the interior of the historical church is decorated with subtle paintings.

The city guests' favorite place is the Resort Park. It is located in the city center. The park started to be established in 1895. At the beginning of the 20th century, the hiking routes in the park had a length of 20 km. Now, it is even much bigger. Today, in the park, you can admire magnificent age-old trees, decorative plants, and several historic constructions preserved on its territory. This wonderful park is very interesting at any time of the year.

There is the Museum of Truskavets Resort in one of the central city streets. It occupies the spectacular villa of the beginning of the 20th century. In seven rooms of the villa, you can see hundreds of unique exhibits, most of which date back to the Middle Ages. The most valuable exhibits are architectural artifacts found when the surroundings of the resort were explored. In several rooms of the museum, temporary themed exhibitions are regularly held.

Art connoisseurs should certainly visit the M. Bilas Art Museum that was opened not so long ago, in 1992. The museum occupies one of the most beautiful wooden buildings in the city that was constructed in the late 19th century. One of the main features of the museum is that it was found when the eminent artist was still alive. Besides Michael

Bilas' paintings, you can see here his personal items and themed exhibits dedicated to his art.

The Pump-Room № 1 is also very popular with visitors of the resort. It was founded in the pre-war period and is located in the city center. The pump-room is distinguished by a spectacular exterior and interior. Here, you can taste different types of mineral water from wells located in the territory of Truskavets. The pump-room is surrounded by the beautiful park with recreation areas.

Vinnytsya

Guide to Vinnytsya

Sightseeing in Vinnytsya what to see. Complete travel guide
Vinnitsa acquired the status of a large-scale modern city only in the 30s of the last century. Now the territory of the city and its immediate vicinity is 4.5% of the total area of Ukraine. It is located in the central part of the Right Bank, on the Dniester River. The history of the picturesque city is more than 600 years old. Today more than 400 thousand people live on its territory. Vinnitsa region has long been a major agricultural region of the country, and this status is preserved for it even now.

The history of the appearance of the name of the city is quite interesting. According to one version, it was named after the Vinnichka River. Many locals have a different version; they believe that their hometown was named Vinnitsa because a few hundred years ago a lot of distilleries were built here. During the excavations on the territory of the city, traces of settlements of Old Russian and Scythian tribes were found, and in the 9th century tribes of Tivertz and ulitsa lived here. Their lands were part of Kievan Rus, and after its devastation they moved to the Galicia-Volyn principality.

In 1362, the Lithuanian army of Prince Olgerd defeated the army of the Tatars, and on these lands, the rapid economic and social development began again. In 1569 the city became part of Poland, whose influence also affected its architectural appearance and lifestyle. It should be noted that Vinnitsa is often mentioned in historical reports as applicable to the events of the National Liberation War, which took place from 1648 to 1654. From 1667, according to the provisions of the Andrusov Truce, the entire territory of Right-Bank Ukraine, including Vinnitsa, was transferred to the power of the Polish crown.

At the end of the XVIII century Vinnitsa experienced one of the most difficult historical periods. More than 1500 of its inhabitants died of plague. Soon the territory of the city passed under the rule of the Russian Empire, and in 1810 about 10 thousand inhabitants already lived in Vinnitsa. In the shortest time, several educational institutions, a hospital, a theater and shops were built in the city. The Great Patriotic War also left a mark in the history of the city. During the war years the number of its inhabitants was reduced by almost 70 thousand, and about 1900 houses were destroyed. In the post-war time, visitors and indigenous people promptly restored the city, restored historical monuments and erected large factories. A beautiful city with a rich history, of course, deserves the attention of curious tourists.

The interesting historical symbol is the old water tower that is located in Kozitskogo Square. The old tower was built of red brick. There is a watch on its facade. In the period of the Second World War, the tower managed to survive even despite the fact that it served as an observation point that time. After the war, there were living quarters in the tower. Families of workers of the local water service company lived here. Since 1984, the tower has belonged to the Local History Museum that houses the collection dedicated to the Afghan war. Near it, there is the Local History Museum itself. You can see these two museums during the single sightseeing tour.

The unique architectural monument is the Manor House of Potocki. At one time, it belonged to a wealthy and influential family. This house is second to none in its beauty and size. It houses unique collections of pieces of art and antique furniture. This luxurious architectural complex has been partially preserved to this day. Now, you can see several restored outbuildings and a mausoleum where the members of the Potockis are buried. All the buildings were destroyed in the 20s of the last century and a new hospital was built here.

In the surroundings of Vinnytsia, there is an important monument dedicated to the Second World War, the Werewolf Bunker. In 1941, the new military complex of Adolf Hitler started to be built and finished in just a year. In total, this complex consists of over 80 ground facilities and 6 underground ones. When Hitler's army retreated, all the ground facilities were destroyed. Underground rooms are being investigated now. A lot of incredible stories and legends are connected with the ruins of the military bunker.

All sweet-teeth should certainly visit the Chocolate Museum that was called after the local Roshen chocolate factory. The museum is located right on the territory of the fabric. It was opened in 2010. Its collection will primarily attract children. During the excursion, they will learn about how different sweets are produced. The significant part of the museum collection is automated, which makes it a unique culture center

Culture: sights to visit
Culture of Vinnytsya. Places to visit old town, temples, theaters, museums and palaces
First and foremost, in Vinnitsa you need to look at the Arch in the Central Park of Culture and Leisure named after Gorky, as well as a fire tower located in the park named after Kozitsky. These historical

memorials are considered a signature of the city. In Vinnitsa, a huge number of museums have been opened, especially the Pirogov Manor-Estate Museum, A. Brusilov's House-Museum and the House-Museum of the legendary writer Kotsyubinsky. All of them, as invaluable exhibits, represent belongings of outstanding citizens and tell visitors about their achievements.

In Vinnitsa several ancient religious buildings, which belong to the XVII-XVIII centuries, were miraculously preserved. In the center of the city is the Holy Transfiguration Cathedral, one of the most beautiful architectural structures of Vinnitsa. For those who are interested in the architectural traditions of the past, it will be interesting to see the Jesuit Monastery, located nearby. The Church of the Blessed Virgin Mary of Angels, built in the middle of the 18th century, deserves special attention. In 1595 in the city, the church of St. Florian, which surprises with its exquisite beauty and unique design, was built.

Among the old buildings that survived during the Great Patriotic War, are the Grocholski manor which is a remarkable monument of the 18th century, and the historic "Savoy" Hotel, which was built in 1912. The architectural monument of the later period is the house of Captain Chetkov. Its construction took place at the beginning of the twentieth century. Also worth seeing are a complex of buildings and a huge park of the hospital named after academician A. Yushchenko; this is a vivid architectural monument of the late 19th century.

In Vinnitsa the old Jewish quarter, located not far from the present city center, has been preserved unchanged. Walking along its attractive streets will become a real journey into the past. Here is located the Shargorod synagogue - one of the most beautiful architectural monuments of the Jewish community. In the early XX century it was closed, and the building requisitioned by the authorities. Another unique attraction is the fountain "Roshen" - it is the largest light and music fountain in the world, which is built on an open reservoir. There are hundreds of interesting places to visit in the city, so lovers of excursions and walks in historical areas among many cities in the country, are increasingly choosing it Vinnitsa.

Attractions & nightlife

City break in Vinnytsya. Active leisure ideas for Vinnytsya - attractions, recreation and nightlife
Guests of the city can successfully combine walks in historical places with other interesting entertainments. In Vinnitsa there is an excellent paintball club "Sparta", where all conditions for a comfortable and interesting stay are created. Also worth highlighting is the Ice Arena, which is a permanent venue for various sport competitions. Here, vacationers can not only see the competitions, but also skate; the sports center has its own rental office. The ice quality here is excellent and the skating rink is designed for 250 people.

Those that prefer to have fun not only during the day, but also at night, will find it interesting to visit the stylish and bright night club "Feride", located in the shopping and entertainment center "Faride Plaza". In Vinnitsa there is another no less attractive and often visited club - "Planet Fashion-Bar". Here, well-known musical groups come to perform.

"Amagamu" entertainment complex can be distinguished among the well-known and visited institutions. Here you can play bowling, as well as relax in a modern nightclub. Every two weeks here, original themed parties with the participation of famous DJs and artists from Ukraine and Russia is held. It should be noted that the entertainment complex was opened only recently, but it quickly gained popularity among local youth.

A few kilometers from Vinnitsa are excellent sanatoriums. They are in demand among fans of a quiet and secluded holiday. Here you can perfectly relax from the city bustle, enjoy the clean air and magnificent scenery. The largest shopping mall in the city is "Megamall". Its visitors can shop all day and relax in specially equipped areas. In the center there are special recreation areas with slot machines for children. For those who local shops do not seem to be enough, they should go to the shopping center "Dastor", which includes shops of very different specialization.

One of the newest and most visited is the Shopping and entertainment center "MagiGrand". Shopping enthusiasts are attracted by numerous shops, and McDonald's is more popular among young In front of the complex is a beautiful square with benches and walkways.

Cuisine & restaurants

Cuisine of Vinnytsya for gourmets. Places for dinner best restaurants Many travelers who come to Vinnitsa are eager to try the dishes of real Ukrainian cuisine; there are more than enough attractive national restaurants in the city. First and foremost, gourmets should pay a visit to the "gastronomic pearl" of Vinnitsa - the restaurant "Kazatskii stan". It is styled as an old Cossack fortress. The atmosphere of past years reigning in the restaurant will make the vacation even more interesting and memorable. They adhere to the old traditions; for guests there is always live music. Visitors of the restaurant can try real Ukrainian dishes cooked according to national recipes in accordance with the best traditions of Ukrainian cuisine.

An equally attractive national restaurant is "Dikanka". This popular establishment offers travelers a chance to relax in a hassle-free homey atmosphere; the stylish menu will impress even big connoisseurs of Ukrainian cuisine. Among the signature dishes of the restaurant are pickled herring, homemade sausage, deruny, as well as real Ukrainian borsch, whose tempting aroma is simply impossible to resist.

Among the popular gastronomic institutions, it is necessary to highlight the restaurant "Auto Grill Myslyvets". They cook not only Ukrainian dishes, but also popular European treats. In the extensive menu you can find a lot of interesting author's dishes, as well as delicious dishes cooked on the grill. For those who are not indifferent to aromatic pilaf and other popular dishes of Uzbek cuisine, it is worth looking into the restaurant "Andijan". Its location is a very attractive modern building, built in the style of past centuries.

In the center of the city there is a stylish restaurant "Tet-a-tet", which will please the guests not only with a smart choice of dishes of regional cuisine, but also an abundance of magnificent author's desserts. In addition to signature pies and cakes, vacationers are offered a decent choice of varieties of fragrant coffee and tea. Economical travelers and business tourists demand the restaurant "Burger Club", whose name speaks for it. In the daytime in its spacious hall there is always a quiet atmosphere, and therefore this cozy place is perfect for organizing business meetings. For serene rest, the "Margate" Cafe is ideal, and here you can also order a lot of interesting dishes at the most attractive prices.

Traditions & lifestyle

Colors of Vinnytsya traditions, festivals, mentality and lifestyle
In Vinnitsa, many competitions, original exhibitions and colorful youth festivals take place every year. With the participation of youth

organizations, very symbolic and beautiful activities are organized in the city, recently a good tradition has been the ornamentation of trees in the city center with the flags of sister cities. Walking in the center, you can see fluttering flags of different cities, including Kielce (Poland), Birmingham (Great Britain), Peterborough (England), Bursa (Turkey), Lipetsk (Russia) and Ribnita (Moldova).

It is youth festivals that make up a significant part of the cultural calendar of the city. They are devoted to a wide variety of topics and unique; in 2013 the festival "HobbyFEST" was held for the first time in the city. As you can guess by the name, the festival is devoted to diverse hobby; people with different hobbies took part in it. The place of the celebration was one of the famous city hotels. For several days in specially equipped halls master classes on different types of creativity and interesting exhibitions were held. The organizers of the festival were local youth organizations. The festival was very successful and added to the already rich cultural calendar of Vinnitsa.

Melomanov in the picturesque Ukrainian city attracts another bright event - the WOODSTOCK festival. This musical festival is well-known to the inhabitants of European countries, and for the first time it was held in Woodstock in 1968. Vinnitsa was the first to hold the music festival in 2012, since then it was decided that this bright musical event be held here every year. Performers and musical groups from different countries of Europe take part in the festival; especially for large-scale events in the city, they equipped a huge open-air stage. Tourists, who are not indifferent to music, should go on vacation in Vinnitsa in late August.

Vinnitsa is a tolerant city, where there is place for any religion. It is often visited by Islamic scholars from Egypt and Saudi Arabia, here they jointly read prayers, and teach local Muslims to read the Holy Quran. Travelers who visit Vinnitsa will be pleasantly surprised by the friendly attitude of locals and their respectful attitude to the cultures and traditions of other countries. Here, every tourist will feel welcome.

Tips for tourists

Preparing your trip to Vinnytsya: advices & hints things to do and to obey

1. Travelers planning a rich excursion program should definitely go to the Southern Bug and visit the Pirogov Manor-Estate, which is considered one of the most interesting sights of Ukraine.

2. Curious tourists will be interested to visit the railway station of Vinnitsa, which recently underwent a large-scale restoration. It is an important historical attraction and has preserved many of the attributes of the past. There is even a machine with carbonated water and a faceted glass - a bright symbol of the Soviet era.

3. In the historical area of Vinnitsa, it is best to walk on foot. Interesting tourist sites here are located in the literal sense, at every step. The historical area is quite compact and quiet, so it's ideal for walking.

4. Locals are very sensitive to their city; its picturesque streets are strikingly clean. Guests from other cities and countries should treat local customs with respect and throw out garbage exclusively in specially designated places; urns are installed in all streets.

5. An unusual city attraction is a tram; its route passes through the most picturesque places of the city. Ride on a tram is suggested for those who have limited time and want to get acquainted with the most important historical symbols of the city.

6. There are several picturesque parks next to the City Council building. During walks through the parks, you can see a huge number of people with laptops and other gadgets that have access to the Internet. The fact is that in the territory of local parks there is free Wi-Fi.

7. A significant part of the city's cafes and restaurants closes early; it is worth taking into account, lovers of late dinners. One of the last to close is McDonald's, as well as restaurants located on the territory of large hotel complexes.

8. Vinnitsa is a pretty quiet city, and therefore you can walk around the central streets without fear, even in the evening. Exploring remote areas of the city is better in the daytime; on holidays do not forget about the elementary measures of caution

Yalta

Guide to Yalta

Sightseeing in Yalta what to see. Complete travel guide
Many travelers associate the enchanting Crimean city with the hot sun, wonderful beaches, picturesque nature, and incomparable architectural monuments. These thoughts are absolutely true. Yalta is a wonderful city for those who want to relax in a beautiful and romantic place. Yalta is the most popular and most famous Crimean resort. It is a picturesque port city that started to attract travelers from other countries over a century ago.

The first references to the city date back to the middle of the 12th century. For a hundred years, its culture has gained a lot of new facets and has been reflected in amazing historical monuments. Yalta attracts fans of beach and ecotourism but fans of sightseeing tourist won't be bored here too. Travelers have a wide choice of places for pleasant recreation, for example, enchanting city beaches and squares.

Remarkably, almost all the beaches of Yalta were paid until 2010. Now, the entrance to them is absolutely free. There can be extra charge only for beach equipment. With it, the biggest part of the coast is distinguished by very good equipment. In 2012, a range of Yalta beaches earned honorary awards for high environmental indicators, which made the resort more attractive. Active travelers can hike through the woods and mountainous areas. The acquaintance with local flora and fauna is also an excellent way to diversify your recreation.

When admiring the panorama of the resort from a birds-eye view, you can see that there are lush green plantings literally a step away from the coast. To enjoy the soft sea and unique nature, it is not necessary to leave the resort, as everything here is within walking distance.

In Yalta, there is a wide choice of boarding houses and sanatoriums, so the guests of the resort have an excellent opportunity to have a wonderful vacation with a profit to their health. Yalta is unique in offering wonderful conditions for recreation of fans of different types of tourism. Eco, health, beach, food, sports and extreme tourism people with different interests and financial possibilities love vacationing here. The resort has been gaining its flawless reputation for many decades. Today, it is one of the most attractive tourist places in the territory of Ukraine and the former CIS countries.

Undoubtedly, the main historic symbol of Yalta is the fascinating old castle with the romantic name "The Swallow's Nest". It was built on top of the bluff rock at the beginning of the 20th century. Originally, the castle belonged to Baron von Stengel. The rich baron wanted his luxurious house to look like German castles. Before the Revolution of 1917, the castle had been in private ownership. After the Revolution, it was nationalized. The castle was damaged significantly by the earthquake in 1927. Then, the historical monument was abandoned. It was restored and recognized as a monument of national significance not so long ago.

Another popular historical site is Livadia Palace that was built at the beginning of the 20th century too. In the 19th century, the first royal residence was built at the site of the palace. Consequently, it was rebuilt completely upon the order of Emperor Nickolas II. He was really impressed by luxurious Italian residences. When he returned from Italy, the Russian Emperor wanted to build the one in his homeland. Today, the guests of Yalta can see the same palace as it was like in the period of the reign of Nickolas II.

The unique monument in the arabesque style is the Dulber Palace. It was built for Petr Romanov. After the Revolution, the palace was rebuilt into a jail where the representatives of the royal family were detained. It was restored completely not so long ago. There is a beautiful landscape garden around the palace.

The wonderful Massandra Palace is a monument in French style. It was built for Count Vorontsov. The palace had not been finished when the count lived. Consequently, it was being built under the guidance of Emperor Alexander III. Like many other royal residences, the Massandra Palace went through several rough historical periods after the Revolution. You can learn about that time during the excursion.

The most significant religious monument in Yalta is the Cathedral of St. Prince Alexander Nevsky. It was built at the beginning of the 20th century and is a unique architectural monument. Its design in Byzantium style makes it very special. The cathedral has preserved beautiful paintings and religious relics. It is located on the territory of the picturesque park.

Top sightseeing
Top architectural sightseeing and landmarks of Yalta ideas on city exploration routes
Swallow Nest, Livadia Palace, Massandra Palace, and Glory Hill are the architectural landmarks, the names of which always remind you the words 'Yalta' and 'Ukraine'. And this is natural, since these prominent landmarks are the ones that shape the historical and architectural look of Yalta. Let's look at these landmarks from high above, namely, from a bird's eye view click the video and make a flight over the architectural ensemble of Yalta. In the main article, you can also read the most interesting facts about every famous landmark of Yalta.

Swallow Nest, Yalta

Facts: » There is a palace on the steep 40-meter cliff. Originally, it was a single-storey building. It was located at the edge of the rock.

» The first owner was the General in 1878. Late, the stone building was built when the landlord changed.

» You can see it on the cards of the early 20 century.

» The 12-meter building withstood the earthquake in 1927. It was refurbished completely only in the late 60s. The foundation of the Swallow Nest hanging above the water was improved. It would collapse into the sea otherwise. Now, the building is earthquake-proof due to banding constructions. The interior has changed little too.

» The part of the building goes off the edge of the steep cliff. It really resembles a nest woven by birds and attached to the edge.

» There is an observation platform in front of the castle. When you go down 1 200 steps, you can reach the local attraction with towers, high spires, and elongated narrow windows.

» Several feature films were shot in the midst of the unusual building.

» Artist Aivazovsky loved painting this whimsical house.

» In September 2011, the final of the international diving competition was held here.

Livadia Palace, Yalta

Facts: » The royal family often visited the summer residence at the Crimean coast.

» On the second floor, there is a permanent exhibition in the room where the nobles stayed. The interior of the rooms has been restored according to preserved pictures.

» Five rooms are open for visitors. The spacious but not luxurious room with a lot of light belonged to Nicholas II. He did not love pretentiousness. The room of the hostess was served as a living room where relatives got together. There is preserved original finish, pieces of furniture, flowerpots, picturesque canvasses, and the piano. The Empress played it.

» The luxurious spouses' bedroom impresses with its luxurious interior. The furniture here is maple. The bed is covered with an ornate silk canopy.

» There is a small dining room finished with yew. In the princesses' classroom, there is a blackboard with inscriptions made by one of the girls.

» The other exhibition is dedicated to the Yalta Conference. The Livadia Palace met the level of the international meeting. Pictures of world leaders taken on the background of the magnificent landscape appeared in all the media of that period.

» In 1834, the Polish Count constructed the first building. The Livadia attraction is over 100 years old.

Massandra Palace, Yalta

Facts: » In 1880, the two-storey palace started to be built for the son of statesman M. Vorontsov.

» Later, the building came to Alexander III. Then, the third level was completed. The exterior was more luxurious. The Massandra building served as a hunting lodge more than a place of permanent residence.

» When the monarch's power was overthrown, the palace was nationalized and used as a hospital for TB patients. Then, there was a winery served as a summer cottage for party officials. The palace turned into a museum about 30 years ago.

» The interior of the house dates back to the 19th century. When viewing two levels, visitors can see offices, audience halls, and private rooms of former landlords. The furniture was carefully selected. It serves all its intended purposes.

» Each room is designed in its own style. There are a lot of famous Russian artists' paintings. You can also see portraits of the imperial family. Porcelain items (vases, tools, and other dishes) were created over 200 years ago.

» At the third level, there is an art exhibition with paintings and sculptures of masters of the 40s-50s of the 20th century.

Glory Hill, Yalta

Facts: » The memorial complex is surrounded by a massive reinforced concrete structure with a white finish covered with Inkerman stone. It's meant to perpetuate the heroism of those killed in the battles of the south coast during the civil and patriotic wars.

» The authors of the memorial built it in the form of a ring. It seems that the changing faces reflect different historical milestones of the country.

» The heroism of partisans and red guards is described in the inscriptions on external limestone-clad walls. There are bas-relief outlines of sailors and soldiers on them.

» The centerpiece of the site is the Eternal Flame. It was lit from the flames of fire on Malakhov Barrow in Sevastopol.

» A hill was specially leveled for the prominent place. You can climb to it using cable railway or an asphalted 2.5-kilometre road. Then you need to go up the stairs to the top of the hill.

» A granite stela is installed at the bottom of the stairway. The funeral sign has the names of battle participants.

» The foundation of the monument is a steel reinforced frame filled with concrete.

» On Victory Day (9 May), a rally and a solemn wreath-laying ceremony are traditionally organized here.

Roman Catholic Church, Yalta

Facts: » There is the Roman Catholic Church near the city embankment. It was built in 1906.

» The church was constructed at the expense of 500 parishioners of the commune. Before, the construction was ceased due to the authorities' disagreement. The paperwork had been prepared for 10 years. The project of the building was offered by architect N. Krasnov. The exterior and interior are characterized by strictness.

» The temple was opened in 1928. Then, other companies rented it and it served as a gymnasium, a showroom, and a museum.

» In the late 20th century, the organ was placed in the hall. The musical instrument was presented by the company from Czechoslovakia. It has 2 200 pipes and 34 registers.

» Today, the church can accommodate up to 200 worshipers.

» The building resembles an elongated cross from the outside. It was built of light gray cutstone blocks. There are no chapels and spires. Stone columns are covered with artificial marble. The floor is made of the same stone but is also polished. The windows are stained glass. There are six rooms in the building.

» There is a molded rose above the front door. You can see the inscription saying that the church is dedicated to God and the Virgin Mary.

Villa Elena, Yalta

Facts: » In 1907, the five-storey hotel was purchased by the merchant from Saratov. He was not satisfied with its exterior but he decided to rebuild the house completely. It was completed in 1912.

» Villa Elena stands out of similar hotels with its height (it was the highest construction in Yalta at that time), a lift, amenities, and the central heating. Each room had water pipelines. The wife of the landlord welcomed many eminent people here.

» You can find the details about Villa Elena located near the shore in the Guidebook of 1913.

» The spacious observation platform has a view of the sea and the mountain range. Southern balconies have a marvelous panoramic view of the landscape garden.

» The Soviet government nationalized the building. The room served as a sanatorium and a hospital of the resort.

» Today, it is officially called Villa Elena Hotel & Residences. It is a five-star hotel.

» This place is also famous for the fact that it is visited by famous domestic and foreign people. It also opens its doors for delegations from different countries.

» There are 32 well-equipped rooms, an audience hall, a restaurant, and a spa.

Vorontsov Palace, Yalta

Facts: » There is a palace at the foot of the mount. It is surrounded by a parking area.

» The staircase leading to the front entrance has a view of the Black Sea. It is surrounded by statues of lions at the sides. They were made by an Italian sculptor.

» The owner of the construction was the legendary Prince, Mikhail

Vorontsov who contributed much to the Russian government. When he died, the building came to the General's relatives.

» The building was built by serfs in1828-1848. Stonecutters manually processed dunstone produced from the nearby rock. It is harder than granite. To level the terrace off, a stone ledge was blown up.

» The complex consists of five separate buildings: Canteen, Central and Guest Buildings, billiard room, rooms for servants and household purposes.

» The palace looks like an impregnable fortress. The botanical garden adds a picturesque view to it.

» Designers were invited to work on its landscape. Mostly coniferous trees grow here. So, the parking area is evergreen in any season. In summer, you can see exotic plants here. Cercis with bright purple florets are especially attractive.

» In the Winter Garden, you can even see ficus that has been growing here since 1838.

Yevpatoriya

Guide to Yevpatoriya

Sightseeing in Yevpatoriya what to see. Complete travel guide
Not everyone knows that Yevpatoria is one of the oldest cities in the world. Every street of the charming city is saturated with the incredible spirit of past centuries. For those who wish to fully appreciate the historical heritage of the city, it is worth paying

attention to the popular hiking route, which is called Little Jerusalem. If you walk along this route, you can see six unique religious sights, as well as a host of other historical sites. The route includes several ancient Turkish baths and handicraft workshops, where even now handmade craftsmen make a variety of handicrafts.

The history of Yevpatoria is incredibly interesting. Originally the settlement based on its place was called Kerkenitida, subsequently Gezlev, and afterwards Yevpatoria. The settlement was founded by the Greeks, and soon it became part of a powerful colony - Chersonesos. The city was perfectly fortified and a fortress was built here with twelve powerful towers. Seven centuries of successful existence of the beautiful Greek city ended suddenly - all residents left the city after learning about the threat of the Sarmatian invasion.

The surviving part of the towers and fortress walls, located on Duvanovskaya Street, today reminds of one of the most important periods in the history of the city. The next historical period concerns Turkish rule. At that time the city was called Gezlev. It had an important strategic importance and was an impeccably fortified settlement with a powerful garrison, where a significant part of the Turkish army was based.

When the Russian-Turkish war ended, and Crimea officially came under the rule of the Russian Empire, the city was renamed Yevpatoria. It was named after the famous Pontus king Mitridat

Yevpator, who repeatedly saved the ancient Kerkinitid from the formidable Scythian tribes. In 1907, between Yevpatoria and Simferopol, the first telephone line was connected, and seven years later the first and the only tramway started to run here on the Crimean coast. The popularity of the resort over time only grew, and so in 1915 passenger trains began to come here. In Soviet times, Yevpatoria was a recognized children's health resort. Many sanatoriums were built here, which were oriented, first of all, to children's recreation and health improvement. Now Yevpatoria is one of the most popular cities in Crimea, which is famous for its developed infrastructure and rich historical heritage.

Among architectural monuments of the Middle Ages, the Gyozlyovsky Gate is worth being mentioned. It was built in the 15th century and was included in the system of city fortifications. The old gate is one of the few fortifications that have been preserved to this day. Over the last hundred years, little attention has been paid to this historical monument, so the gate was destroyed almost completely in the 50s of the last century. After a few years, the city government decided to restore this monument and finished it in 2004.

Unique Muslim monuments, including the Dervish Tekke, have been preserved too. This architectural complex is a very unique place in Crimea. It includes the building of the old mosque, tekke, madrasah, and some other constructions built in the period between the 15th and 18th centuries. In the 30s of the last century, all the religious constructions lost their original status and were used for the fleet's needs. In 2000, the architectural complex started to be reconstructed for the first time.

The most beautiful Muslim monument in Yevpatoria is the Juma-Jami Mosque. It was built in the 16th century and reconstructed for many times. Despite the fact that the mosque has almost lost its original appearance, it is still a vivid representation of historical traditions. In the Soviet period, the mosque served as a museum. It gained its religious status back only in the 90s of the last centuries.

The unique architectural monument in Greek style is the Temple of St. Elijah built at the beginning of the 20th century. The temple is distinguished by its very beautiful facade, on which you can see a lot of arches and elements in Greek and Byzantium style. The main values of the temple's interior are fascinating stained glass windows that look very interesting in the sun. Several years ago, this temple was reconstructed too and then was presented in all its glory. The temple is surrounded by a small garden and you can walk through it after taking an excursion.

Culture: sights to visit

Culture of Yevpatoriya. Places to visit old town, temples, theaters, museums and palaces

Yevpatoria is a city of contrasts, which never ceases to amaze guests with its irresistible modern appearance and amazing historical atmosphere. It impresses with its elegant medieval architecture and modernity. Religious tolerance and morals inherent in locals never differ in a mild character. Those who are going to devote rest to the study of historical monuments in Yevpatoria will not be exactly bored.

The most important sights of the city are the famous "Juma-Jama Mosque". It is a surprisingly beautiful architectural structure. The beautiful Cathedral of St. Nicholas the Wonderworker is also an important symbol of the city, and the Yeghia-Kapai synagogue reminds locals and guests of the resort about one of the most important historical periods. A lot of impressions will be presented by a walk along the winding streets of the Old Town. There are historical monuments on the Gorky Embankment, as well as on the theater square.

Very interesting in architectural plan is the building of the theater A.C. Pushkin and the gymnasium named after Selvinsky. Also in Yevpatoria there are many notable monuments, for example, a monument to Semyon Duvan - one of the mayors who managed to turn Yevpatoria from a remote provincial town to a resort of international importance at the beginning of the 20th century. There is also a monument to Major-General Nikolai Tokarev, a hero of the Great Patriotic War. Also famous in the city is the local poet of the XVII century Ashik Omer, who was born in Yevpatoria and all his life accompanied the Ottoman army in her numerous campaigns.

The resort town is not deprived of curious cultural institutions. It is worth visiting the Pharmacy Museum and the Mail Museum, which over the years has managed to collect excellent collections of exhibits. Important historical facilities of the middle Ages are the Turkish baths, which have not ceased to function for several hundred years. The fortress gates, which are located not far from the embankment deserves special attention. They are the surviving part of the ancient fortress, which for many years defended the city and its inhabitants from numerous conquerors. Despite the fact that Yevpatoria has always been a primary goal in the eyes of the latter, the city managed to preserve the historical heritage of various epochs, from the time of antiquity to the rich innovations of the 19th century.

Attractions & nightlife

City break in Yevpatoriya. Active leisure ideas for Yevpatoriya attractions, recreation and nightlife
In the holiday season, the most popular vacation spots are the embankment and the Frunze Park. There are always a lot of people here; even late at night on the embankment you can meet couples strolling leisurely. It often hosts various concerts, festivals, and sometimes sports events. In the off-season, as well as at the height of hot summer, the embankment remains an excellent place for hiking,

many guests of the resort they remain a favorite entertainment. If you go to the sea through Frunze Street, you can find a pump-room of mineral water on the way, where everyone can try therapeutic water.

Fans of outdoor activities will certainly like the "Avangard" stadium, where a wonderful modern go-kart functions. For tourists trips to interesting natural attractions are arranged, during which they can appreciate the unique nature of these fertile places. At the intersection of Pushkin and Frunze streets a magnificent arboretum begins, so you can enjoy the natural splendor without leaving the resort. In summer, attractions for children are always installed on the territory of a beautiful park.

The main value of the resort is beautiful beaches, where you can swim practically all year round. The most popular and lively beaches are located next to the walkway, where vacationers are offered diverse leisure activities with the most unusual entertainment. On a hot day you can have a great time in the Frunze Park, where you will especially enjoy resting for children. Here for the little tourists is equipped a wonderful Old Fortress, fairy town, a huge Ferris wheel, different roundabouts and swings. In the park you can ride a train or rent a bicycle. There is also a children's cafe where amusing clowns entertain young guests.

In Yevpatoria there is a beautiful water park "banana republic", as well as a very interesting aquarium with a diverse entertainment program.

Fans of loud music and dancing till dawn will be attracted by the night club Malibu Ultra. You can also go on vacation to the stylish club "Amsterdam". For those who wish to spend an evening in a romantic atmosphere, it is worth renting a yacht or a boat and making an unforgettable sea trip. Fans of shopping on vacation, too, will not be bored. They will be pleased with a decent selection of modern shops and countless colorful souvenir shops.

Cuisine & restaurants

Cuisine of Yevpatoriya for gourmets. Places for dinner best restaurants

People began to settle on the territory of modern Crimea since ancient times. The formation of local culinary traditions was influenced by representatives of a variety of nationalities. Travelers, who will rest in Yevpatoria, should pay special attention to the Karaite and Tatar cuisine. Karaite is one of the oldest Crimean cattle breeding tribes, who led a predominantly nomadic way of life, which inevitably affected their kitchen.

In restaurants and cafes in Yevpatoria which specialize in cooking national cuisine, you can try a lot of interesting lamb foods, as well as excellent pastries. Dishes of local cuisine are quite hearty and nutritious, and therefore you can even get satisfied on half of your generous portion. Many vegetable dishes here are also prepared with the addition of meat; a fairly common meal is pilaf with mutton.

An important element of the national menu is the first dishes, based on the rich meat broth. Dishes of Karaite cuisine do not differ simply. For cooking many classical treats cook have to spend several hours. Fans of meat delicacies should definitely try dried lamb, which is considered one of the most delicious dishes of local cuisine; it is cooked according to old recipes. National cuisine is not limited to only meat treats; an important place is given to dairy products. As many years ago, today in Yevpatoria delicious cheeses are prepared, and with addition of milk mass of original sweets are prepared too.

If we talk about desserts, then it is worth mentioning Karaite halva. Very interesting sweets are cooked with honey, nuts and milk. Sea cuisine is represented here in varieties, so the lovers of fish dishes and sea delicacies will definitely enjoy a vacation in Yevpatoria. Practically in any cafe it is possible to try not only the most delicious Black Sea fish, but also squid, rapans, mussels and crabs. Pleasure is not cheap, but it is definitely worth it. The most popular fish restaurants and cafes are located on the waterfront. The resort presents gastronomic establishments of various directions, so fans of Ukrainian, Russian, European and Oriental cuisine can easily find a great place to relax.

Tips for tourists

Preparing your trip to Yevpatoriya: advices & hints things to do and to obey

1. From the railway and bus stations you can get to any resort area by public transport, the most common type of which is a fixed-route taxi. It is not advisable to use the services of ordinary taxi drivers, who are on duty at city stations; the cost of their services is very high.

2. Yevpatoria is a pretty quiet resort, so you can walk around the embankment and the central streets without fear, even at night. At the same time, do not forget about the elementary measures of caution. To take valuables with you for a walk without the need, is not worth it.

3. One of the most common problems is pocket thieves, so in crowded places you should pay close attention to personal things. You cannot leave things unattended on the beach, in restaurants and cafes.

4. Exchange of currency is recommended only in banks or private exchange offices, and from private services it is best to refuse - there is a high probability of becoming a victim of scammers. Fans of beach holidays should not forget that the sun in Crimea is very hot. Going on a trip, you must take with you all possible means of protection from the sun. They should also be used by those who expect to just walk around the city for a long time.

6. In addition to fixed-route taxis, trams are a popular form of public transport; their network covers all areas of the city. It should be noted

that the tram is also the cheapest mode of transport, a trip by shuttle bus will cost twice as much.

7. The resort presents both free and paid beaches, the latter are distinguished by excellent equipment. For a modest fee, you can access a luxurious beach with changing cabins, showers and charming fountains with fresh water.

8. Local catering establishments will please vacationers with affordable prices. The most expensive and prestigious restaurants are located on the waterfront, and on the streets of the city you can find a lot of excellent cheap cafes and canteens.

9. The choice of places for accommodation for the guests of Yevpatoria is huge. There are excellent hotels and guesthouses, sanatoriums and boarding houses here, private apartments and cottages are very popular with holidaymakers. All types of housing are characterized by a common feature - the closer the location to the sea, the higher the cost of accommodation.

Zaporozhye

Guide to Zaporozhye

Sightseeing in Zaporozhye what to see. Complete travel guide
Zaporizhia - one of the most beautiful and ancient cities of Ukraine, whose territory's settlement began in the era of the Early Paleolithic. Scientists have discovered on these lands traces of more than a

hundred settlements and valuable artifacts of the Bronze Age. On these lands, the mighty Scythian kingdom was founded and existed for several hundred years. On the Scythian dominion, now are the remaining burial mounds and statues that bring to mind the famous Polovtsian women, who symbolized the invincibility and immortality of the Scythian warriors. These statues were sacrificed by soldiers, because they believed that they guarded them and brought good luck in battle.

After the defeat of the Scythian kingdom, these lands were captured by the Huns, Avars and Khazars. Very soon the Russian prince Svyatoslav defeated the Khazars, and after him the Pechenegs came to the lands of modern Zaporizhia. About this intense period of history, also recall an important landmark, on Voznesenovskiy descent there is a monument of the glorious prince Svyatoslav. Already from the middle of the 11th century these lands were taken by the Polovtsian tribe. The Russian princes did not manage to break the Polovtsian troops, as the Mongol-Tatar invasion struck Russia.

The history of Zaporizhia is inextricably linked with the famous Zaporozhye Sich, about which there were legends. The Cossacks living here were not only brave warriors; they were an independent army, which was subordinate only to its ataman. In fact, it was an army of robbers who believed that all the prey that was lost in battle was legal. The life and traditions of the Cossacks had a great influence on the formation of the culture of the city, some echoes of long-gone times are still manifesting even now.

The history of Zaporizhia as a city began with the formation of the Novorossiysk province, which was held by the decree of Catherine the Great. In the place of the modern city, the Empress ordered the founding of the Dnieper defensive line to block the Turkish conquerors from accessing the southern borders of the empire. The largest fortress of the line was called Alexandrovskaya. Over the years more and more residential buildings appeared around the fortress, and soon a small defensive point turned into a real city. In 1921, Aleksandrovsk was renamed Zaporizhia, and the city continued to develop actively. Now Zaporizhia is one of the most attractive tourist centers of the country, and tens of thousands of tourists come to admire the unique sights of the city and walk along its picturesque streets every year.

In the city, there are a lot of old beautiful historical and religious monuments. The main religious place in Zaporizhia is the Cathedral of the Protecting Veil of the Mother of God. The first church at its site was built in 1778. A hundred of years ago, it was decided to build a new stone cathedral here. In the first half of the 20th century, it was destroyed completely and restored only in 2007. Now, it is an exact copy of the historic cathedral. The construction is 54 m high.

In one of the most fascinating buildings of the central district, there is the Zaporozhye Regional Art Museum founded in 1971. It will impress admirers of painting. The museum collection includes almost 13 000 exhibits. Here, you can see the paintings of famous Russian artists who lived in the 19th-20th centuries. Besides paintings, the museum presents a big collection of pieces of folk art. In the museum, there are special halls for temporary exhibitions, ten of which, at least, are annually held.

In the city, there is another unique nature attraction the Zaporozhye Oak. The oak is aged over 700 years and impresses with its incredible size. It is 36 m high and its girth is over 6 m. In 1996, the tree was struck by lightning and since that time, it has had only one living branch. The unique tree is an important national attraction. Nowadays, the city government does its best to reserve the oak.

The incredibly beautiful historical building, where the Territorial Council was located, now houses the Zaporozhye Local History Museum. It was founded in 1922. The initiator of its construction was the archeologist Novitsky. Nowadays, the museum presents over 100 000 exhibits, including unique archeological artifacts. The museum stores the big collection of historical weapons, old accessories, and hunting trophies. Most of the exhibits are dedicated to the Zaporozhye Cossacks' history and traditions. Another interesting place is the Weapons History Museum opened not so long ago, in 2004. Today, it houses almost 2 000 cold and fire arms.

Culture: sights to visit

Culture of Zaporozhye. Places to visit - old town, temples, theaters, museums and palaces

Zaporizhia is a large industrial city, one of the most important industrial centers of Ukraine. It does not at all resemble those industrial cities that were actively rebuilt during the Soviet period. Many shady avenues are broken on the banks of the Dnieper, and all the streets of the city, not to mention the parks and squares, are simply buried in the abundance of greenery. Right after DneproGES there is a small area, which locals call Sotsgorod. This is the very realm, where the architectural style, called the Stalinist Empire, rules undividedly. The houses here are all majestic and high, with columns, fountains and porticos, as well as large courtyards.

An important landmark of the city, which will be appreciated by lovers of architecture, is the Glinka concert hall, which simply amazes with its strict, majestic and calm architecture. The real adornment of the city is the "Zaporizhia Ukrainian Music and Drama Theater" named after Magar, whose unusual facade with figures of collective farmers and workers is something pompous, but at the same time very harmonious.

Anyone who did not see the Dnieper was not in Zaporizhia. Its graceful horseshoe-like view is good in any foreshortening, not every city of Ukraine can boast of such attractive and interesting industrial attractions. On both sides of the horseshoe-like view there are two remarkable parks: on the right bank there is the "Energetikov Park" with its ancient poplars and spreading lindens and on the left bank the Metallurgists' Park, very quiet, shady and calm.

In the city there is another important natural monument, from which originates Zaporizhia - the island of Khortytsia - national heritage of all of Ukraine. The island is attractive not only for its Cossack past. It is truly a unique nature reserve, which is not called the pearl of the Dnieper in vain. On the island in miniature are all types of landscapes, which are typical for Ukraine. Here there are steppe, forest-steppe, and floodplains, meadows, and forest, and in the northern part of the island there are even rocks. The vegetable world of Khortytsia is incredibly diverse, and the entire southern part of the island is a protected area. The island is connected with the city by one of the most beautiful bridges in Europe "Preobrazhensky". The historical past of Zaporizhia is rich and multifaceted, even large-scale factories and industrial centers could not eclipse its monuments.

Attractions & nightlife

City break in Zaporozhye. Active leisure ideas for Zaporozhye attractions, recreation and nightlife

As in any large city, in Zaporizhia are accessible the most different centers of leisure and entertainment. A lot of options for active recreation in Zaporizhia are connected with Khortitsa. On the island there are picturesque cycling routes, along which you can travel all day. Vacationers are offered to rent a bicycle or go for a walk on the island, which will also give a lot of impressions. The participants of organized excursions have an opportunity to get to the reserved part of Khortitsa, where you can only walk on foot. Guests of the island are offered a ride and on horseback, this romantic entertainment will not leave anyone indifferent.

The city can offer fans of urban entertainment a decent choice of entertainment centers, shops, discos and nightclubs. The modern shopping and entertainment complex "City Mall" is great for shopping and for family holidays. In addition to numerous clothing stores, the largest supermarket of the city - "Auchan" - is located here. No less popular is the shopping center "Palladium Plaza". In addition to the huge selection of shops, its main distinctive feature is a pleasant interior decoration. In the center, there are several cozy recreation areas and attractive cafes.

Vacationers with children will be interested to visit the entertainment complex "Shekiland", which presents a variety of attractions. There are also children's favorite trampolines, and popular slot machines, as well as mini-train and fun attractions for the youngest. It is noteworthy that the entertainment center operates its own system of award tickets, in case of winning they can be spent on paying for new entertainment.

The "Cosmos City" center offers the city's guests quite an unusual kind of recreation. Its last floor is equipped with a special area for skating for roller skaters, where everyone can perfect their skills. Among the many nightclubs, "Music Hall" stands out; it is an incredibly beautiful and cozy place. Here you can not only listen to your favorite music, dance and watch a regular entertainment program, but also relax in a cozy restaurant. "Music Hall" is a multi functional recreation center, which people of different ages; musical and gastronomic preferences like to visit

Cuisine & restaurants

Cuisine of Zaporozhye for gourmets. Places for dinner best restaurants

Modern Zaporizhia is a city of factories and metallurgists; it is the presence of large industrial enterprises that determines its appearance. In the central area of the city are modern office buildings, as well as a campus, and therefore the concentration of gastronomic institutions is incredibly great. The most visited catering establishments are McDonald's, the restaurant "Kartoplyana Khata", the restaurant "Eurohat", the pizzeria "Pizza Celentano" and "Autopizza". "Mont Blanc" stands out among fast-foods. Among its distinctive features is an extensive menu and affordable prices, it is also worth noting the high quality of its dishes. Numerous kiosks and shopping tents that offer good pancakes, hot dogs or shawarma will come to the aid of adherents of budget tourism.

Those that prefer not to economize on food should pay attention to the restaurant "Bon appétit". It is decorated in the style of the 70s of the last century. The hall of the restaurant is decorated with photographs of famous actors of those years. But this is not the only feature of the institution; guests will be pleased with the decent choice of culinary masterpieces and very attentive service. Fans of all famous Italian treats are sure to be attracted by the restaurant "Autopizza"located at the intersection of Lenina Avenue and Krasnogvardeyskaya Street. It is a cozy establishment with a classic interior and attractive menu.

On the Stalevarov Street, there is a famous restaurant "Eurohat". Signature treats here are incredibly delicious and the menu features dishes exclusively of Ukrainian cuisine. Prices in the restaurant always remain at an attractive level, so the flow of visitors here is great at any time of the day. One of the best fast-food establishments in the city is the "Kartoplyana Khata" restaurant. Waiters here are polite and attentive. In addition to classic national treats, they offer guests interesting dishes of Mexican cuisine to try. The restaurant is decorated in a simple style, so it is quite suitable for organizing a business meeting.

In Zaporizhia you can easily find restaurants of different directions. The city is visited by many foreign guests that cannot be left without attention of local chefs. As in all modern cities of the country, there are international restaurants and the most popular Japanese cuisine.

Major sightseeing
Cultural sights

Cultural sightseeing in Ukraine. What to visit museums, temples, castles and palaces

Ukraine can be proud not only of the fertile soils and expanses of its steppe, but also of its cultural wealth that can be seen by visiting museums, cathedrals, squares and other places that eloquently portray the country's complicated history and demonstrate its culture in all its glory. The National Art Museum of Ukraine which is located in Kiev is the largest art museum in the country. Here guests will see works of Ukrainian artists and masters of several eras: icons, paintings, sculptures and other works of art. The museum organizes guided tours in several languages. There is a souvenir shop and a workshop here, where adults and children are taught to paint pictures.

The National Museum of the History of Ukraine in Kiev is a large, majestic building that holds within its walls historical documents and artifacts from ancient times to the present day. The collection continues to grow still. Here you can see the past of the country, and look at the present through the eyes of modern Ukrainians through photos, weapons, tools, clothing and much more. The unique museum "Pysanka" is located in the city of Kolomyia. Several thousands of beautiful Easter eggs are housed in the building, part of which is a painted egg. The museum is dedicated to the Ukrainian art of decorating Easter eggs, but there are exhibits from all over the world among its collection.

At the border of the Kirovograd region is sited the Strategic Missile Forces Museum. The museum consists of the formerly secret land and underground buildings of the Soviet era that had to do with nuclear weapons. Inside, everything is as it was in those tense times when the officers who were working here were ready to put the weapon into use at any moment. Visitors will be able to control the launch of missiles independently using equipment that simulates a military situation. There is a pharmacy of the 18th century in Lviv, which became a museum in the 1960s. The institution continues to operate simultaneously as a pharmacy and a museum. The large collection of the museum contains ancient medicines and devices, a rare herbarium and other interesting exhibits. You can also buy here "Iron Wine", medicine with iron, useful for blood.

The Museum of Folk Architecture and Life, Uzhhorod Zakarpattia, is not a museum in the usual sense of the word. Here, the guests of Uzhhorod will see not a building with a large collection of exhibits, but many buildings that are themselves exhibits. These are ancient buildings, among which there is a church, residential buildings and a mill. The museum tells about the life of several ethnic groups of

Zakarpattia. There are icons of the 17th century, dishes and other exhibits in the museum. Space enthusiasts should visit the Museum of Cosmonautics named after S. P. Korolev in Zhytomyr. The house-museum of Sergei Pavlovich Korolev, the chief engineer of the Soviet space program, tells about his life. In the main building of the museum there is a huge number of exhibits related to space, among which is lunar soil.

The Jesuit Church in Lviv was built in the 17th century by Catholic monks. Its construction took two decades. Inside the church is decorated with frescoes and sculptures. According to legend, here, in the dungeon, wanders the restless ghost of a monk, who was imprisoned to pray for his transgressions, but instead sold his soul to the Devil. There is the magnificent Holy Annunciation Cathedral in Kharkiv, with beautiful frescoes and icons. It was opened at the very beginning of the last century and still impresses the guests of the city.

The Olesko Castle is located in the Lviv region. In this 14th-century building that stands on a hill, once lived the great polish king John III Sobieski. In the 19th century, it was damaged by an earthquake, after which it was restored. At the moment there is an art museum in the castle with hundreds of wonderful exhibits from the 10th to 18th centuries: paintings, decorations and sculptures. Visitors can find ancient statues in the garden. In Poltava there is a snow-white monument-colonnade called the Rotunda of Peoples Friendship or the

White Gazebo. It was opened in 1909, built in memory of the Battle of Poltava in 1709. The columns look like a horseshoe shape. This is a kind of tribute to the legend, according to which a local resident shod Peter the Great's horse, which decided the outcome of the battle.

The Khotyn Fortress, originally of the 10th century, stands on the bank of the Dniester. It was rebuilt several times till the 16th century. The fortress is interesting not only for its history, but also for a non-drying wet spot on one of the walls. According to one legend, during the siege of the fortress, a girl decided to collect water for the soldiers from the river. As the girl climbed on the wall, the enemies saw her and hit her with arrows, and as a result she splashed some of the water on the wall. According to another version, the prince's daughter was bricked in the wall, as she did not want to marry the man she did not love. It is believed that this stain from her tears would not dry out until the poor prisoner is reunited with her lover.

Festivals in Ukraine

Fun and festivities in Ukraine celebrations, festivals and cultural events

Among the Ukrainian holidays and holiday traditions, there are those well-known to Europeans, for example, the New Year and the First of May holidays. There are also unique holidays, like ceremonies for Ivan Kupala, celebrating Christmas and New Year twice, a new holiday called Day of Defender of Ukraine and interesting traditions of Palm

Sunday. Ukraine combines European traditions, Orthodox Christianity rituals and the pagan heritage of the Eastern Slavs. Holidays are celebrated on a large scale, and pagan as well as orthodox traditions are honored even by faithless Ukrainians.

Ukraine celebrates the New Year with most of the world from the night of December 31st to January 1st. The Christmas trees are decorated in the middle of December. The celebration starts in the evening or in the middle of the day, the table is set with all sorts of dishes. It is impossible to imagine a New Year's celebration without the traditional Olivier salad. Usually, the holiday is celebrated with the family in front of the TV, accompanied with the songs of popular artists. After the striking of the clock, the celebrants go outside to play snowballs and launch fireworks. After the arrival of New Year, the youth tries to meet with friends to continue the holiday celebration. The New Year's symbols are the gray-bearded Santa Claus, dressed in white or blue clothes and traveling by sled with horses, and his granddaughter Snow Maiden, who is represented differently: from a little girl to a young woman.

Ukrainians celebrate Christmas according to the Orthodox calendar, on January 7th. This holiday is not celebrated with such noise and scope as the New Year. During its celebration, pagan rituals can be observed, especially in the countryside. Celebrants, sometimes in masks of animals, go caroling, that is, they go from house to house singing Christmas songs, and the owners of the houses treat them to sweets. It is interesting that from 2017 Ukrainians officially began to celebrate the Catholic Christmas on December 25th, which symbolizes Ukraine's support for European orientation, and the adoption of European values. Anyway, two Christmases sounds great.

The Old New Year is celebrated on the 14th of January. This is not a state public holiday, but it falls on the last days of the New Year breaks. The festivity appeared because of the transition from one calendar to another, between which there is a difference of 13 days. Old New Year is the last chance to have fun before the inevitable end of the holidays. Many faithful Ukrainians celebrate the Day of the Baptism of Russia on the nineteenth of January, by dipping into an ice hole, carved into the form of crosses. It is believed that dipping into an ice water three times in the middle of winter clears a person and heals him of all diseases.

On March 8th, Ukraine celebrates International Women's Day. After the collapse of the USSR, this celebration of equality acquired a completely different meaning. Now it is called "the holiday of beauty and spring", and during the celebration, women of all ages are wished not success and strength, but beauty and femininity. The Great Day, or Easter, is celebrated in April with Easter painted eggs that symbolizes the beginning of life. Ukrainians paint eggs with pleasure in order to break them together later at the table and eat them. The holiday does not do without a sweet Easter cake, which is blessed in the church. 49 days after Easter, Trinity Day is celebrated. People attend services in churches and go to the graves of relatives, where it is common to commemorate the dead, treat themselves to a meal and sometimes drink wine. Many people also leave food at the graves. It is believed that the souls of the dead return to earth on Trinity day and eat the food left at their grave.

The April Palm Week, ending on Palm Sunday, relates to the entry of Jesus into Jerusalem. On Saturday and Sunday, according to the old custom, many Ukrainians beat each other with pussy willow branches to cure diseases and expel evil spirits. In the beginning of May, Ukrainians have a lot of time-out because of the large number of holidays. The first of May is Labor Day. Till the 19th century, spring was celebrated on this day, and from Soviet times, peaceful demonstrations of workers are held on May 1st. May 9th is one of the most important holidays, marking the USSR Victory Day over the Nazis, the end of the war. Parades, meetings with veterans, and special demonstrations are held throughout the country. Old and new war films are broadcasted on television too.

From the end of June to the beginning of July, Ivan Kupala, or the Day of the Summer Solstice is celebrated. According to belief, a fern blossoms during this time. It gives the person who found it the opportunity to find any treasure, an understanding of the language of animals, and other incredible powers. On this holiday, it is customary to jump over bonfires, to tell fortunes through the flower wreaths, and gather herbs. Since 1996, on June 28th, the Constitution Day of Ukraine is celebrated; this holiday was considered by Ukrainians as an important one after the Revolution of 2014. Before that, it did not have much weight, even as a public holiday and a day off. On August 24th, Independence Day from the USSR is celebrated. On this day, a military parade is being held in Kiev, likewise gala concerts are held in many cities of Ukraine. On the 14th of October, the Day of the Defender of Ukraine is celebrated. This is a new holiday, introduced in 2014 because of the Russian invasion of Ukraine. At the same time, the 14th of October is the day of the Ukrainian Cossacks.

Unique sights

Travel ideas for Ukraine unique sights, worth Guinness records

The Temple Of Donators

The Temple of Donators is one of the most important sights of the Crimea. It's located in an incredibly beautiful place, in one of the caves of Eski-Kerman mountains. It's incredibly difficult to find this amazing cave storing priceless religious artifacts. Travelers are advised to go sightseeing with an experienced guide, otherwise there would be a great risk of getting lost in the maze of insurmountable mountains and dense forests. Main features of the ancient cave temple are primeval murals; according to scientists, they were painted in the 12th century.

According to one version, the temple was founded by a wealthy ducal family, whose name remains unknown. Currently, there is the only pathway that originates in the valley and gradually rises to the entrance of the temple. Despite the fact that the shrine can be seen from afar, it's not easy to find the path leading to it among the dense thickets of trees and a huge number of scarps. Beautiful frescoes and inaccessibility are not the only distinguishing features of the Temple of Donators. Since ancient times, locals believed in miraculous power of these places, which was confirmed by amazing stories of people who have visited the shrine.

Mishor Al Petri

Mishor Al Petri certainly stands out among the most prominent attractions of Crimea; it was opened in 1988. It originates in the foothills of the picturesque village of Mishor and takes passengers to the top of Ai-Petri. The cable car is2,980 meters long. The intermediate station is situated at an altitude of 391 meters, and the terminal station is found at an altitude of 1,153 meters.

Construction of the cable car began in 1967; the original project needed substantial amendments. The country through which Mishor Ai Petri passes is incredibly picturesque and complex at the same time; it was very difficult to organize a cableway along high cliffs. The cable car runs two cabins, each of which can accommodate 35 people.

It would take about 15 minutes to get from the bottom to the terminal station, during which passengers will have an opportunity to appreciate beauty of the surrounding landscapes in full. The top of Mount Ai Petri is equipped with magnificent viewing platforms. These amazing places are very popular among guests of the Crimea. Not everyone knows that Miskhor Ai Petri is mentioned in Guinness World Records. Span between its middle and upper station is the world's longest unsupported span, with a length of more than 2 kilometers.

Pripyat

The Ukrainian city of Pripyat has always been associated with one of the most horrible disasters in the world over the past decade an explosion at the Chernobyl Nuclear Power Plant. That was the construction of the plant that marked the beginning of a new settlement. Pripyat was officially proclaimed a city in 1979 and had grown to a population of more than 47 000 people by the time it was evacuated, seven years later. On April 28, 1986, the very next day after the explosion the "City of Atomic Scientists" was almost empty.

The deserted city is located on the banks of the nearby Pripyat River. The city itself and the surrounding areas have been so badly contaminated by radiation fallout that they were declared a danger zone. The main threat to visitors is radioactive dust that has ingrained in the soil, trees and buildings.

Tourists are attracted to these places by a chance to explore the abandoned buildings. The citizens were leaving so quickly that many of them left a lot of things inside. Pripyat still maintains the status of the city, although no one lives there for a long time. Every year once residents of the city visit their abandoned piece of homeland to meet up with friends and like-minded people who have experienced that terrible tragedy. Traditionally meetings take place in early May. Just for a few days Pripyat comes alive, human voices and traffic sounds are heard through the city.

Optimistic Cave

Literally the most optimistic cave (Optymistytschna cave) in the world is located in Ternopol region, in Ukraine. It has the impressive size. The confused tunnels of the cave have the length of more than 230 km. The Optimistic Cave is the longest peak in the world. The complicated underground labyrinth was discovered in 1966. To date, more than 200 large expeditions have visited the cave.

One of the most striking discoveries of the scientists were the helictites - the unique calcite information. It was formerly thought that the Helictites can develop exclusively in the limestone caves. If the scientists will prove that the complex complex of the underground labyrinths is linked to the neighboring cave by the Optimistic Cave, it becomes one of the greatest speleological discoveries of recent years. In this case, the general length of the cave will be increased to 123 km.

For the convenience of the researchers, about 20 camps were equipped in the underground vaults. The largest and best equipped one is 'Oasis' camp, where about 50 people can recover. It must be mentioned that the Optimistic Cave is not only one of the largest, but also one of the safest caves in the world. The tourists and the participants of the spelaeological children's clubs visit them regularly.

Chernobyl

Nuclear disaster, which happened in 1986 on the Chernobyl plant, is considered one of the greatest ecological catastrophes in human history. Their consequences for the once flourishing industrial city became irreparable. Today Chernobyl is the empty ghost town, which is absolutely unsuitable for life. The huge emission of radioactive pollutants in the explosion became the largest in the whole history of atomic energy. Even today, it is very dangerous to visit the city, as the radiation level is still high.

According to official data, dozens of people have died from radiation. Thousands of people living in the field of damage suffered from oncological diseases. The terrible catastrophe had also added irreparable harm to the reproductive system of humans. The number of inborn pathologies among the children whose parents have experienced the disaster of the Chernobyl plant has increased a hundred times. There were many legends about the terrible mutants living in Chernobyl. Not all of these legends are a brain sprout.

Plant and animals, which can be seen in the city terrarium, look really terrible. Their appearance, to say the least, is unhealthy. There is a lot of effort to find the symmetrical leaf on one of the trees in Chernobyl. The news about the animals mutating in the city are kept secret. Some terrible shots can still be found in the net. One of the most dreadful and dangerous cities in the world attracts the researchers and the scientists, whose main subject is the mutating flora and fauna - the valuable material for the study.

Tunnel of Love

One of the most remarkable and romantic places on earth can be found in the Ukrainian city of Klevan. Its landmark is the Liebestunnel - the three-kilometer long railway track, on both sides of which the tall trees grow. Their crowns are linked together and form an incredibly beautiful corridor. For many years now, the romantic tunnel has attracted photographers from all over the world, as well as the newlyweds, who organize the original and very beautiful photoshootings.

The railway through the tunnel is in operation. Three times a day, the train goes here, which supplies the raw material to the nearby woodworking company. The dense green tunnel of the right arch form is a true botanical phenomenon. No one has ever laid hands on his education. The tunnel is beautiful in all seasons. In late spring and summer, it plays with all shades of green color, and in the autumn is red colored. The natural attraction can also be visited in winter when the tree vaults are covered with snow.

The couples who visit this romantic place have a good tradition. As a testament to fidelity and allegiance, they plant the flowers of the railway, which make the marvelous love tunnel even more romantic. The length of the tunnel is quite large. Some of the railroad tracks around which they have been formed have long since disappeared. These places are as found for walks. Here one can enjoy the beauty and the greatness of nature for hours.

Infected Apartment in Kramatorsk

One of the most egregious cases of radiation detection occurred in the Ukrainian city of Kramatorsk, which now is known throughout the world. The capsule with the radioactive element cesium-137 was detected within the wall of a residential building. The history of this case goes back to 70s of the last century, when an ampoule with cesium was lost during industrial activities in Karanskyi career. One of the large enterprises mined gravel and crushed stone in this quarry. The vial fell out of a measuring device during the planning stage.

An extraction of gravel had to be stopped immediately. The search for the ampoule lasted a week, but ended in failure. That days, the rubble from the quarry was used extensively for the construction of Olympic facilities in Moscow, as well as for building houses in the surrounding cities. Kramatorsk was among those cities too. In1980, a building #7 on Gvardeytsiv Kantemirovtsiv Street was put into operation. The dimensions of the ampoule, which was lost in the 70's are only 8x4 mm; it emitted up to 200 roentgen per hour.

Already in 1980, the residence was fully settled. A year later, a 18-year-old girl, who lived in one of the apartments, suddenly died. In 1982, her 16-year-old brother died too, and then his mother followed them. Even after that, the flat with the radioactive ampoule in a wall didn't attract much of a public attention, despite the fact that all the people died from leukemia. A new family moved into the apartment, and their boy died there too. His father managed to start a detailed investigation, during which the vial was found in the wall. For 9 years, while the ampoule was in the wall, 6 people died and another 17 tenants have been recognized as disabled in the radioactive flat.

Gorge Maryam-Dere

In the immediate vicinity of the Crimean city of Bakhchisaray there is the valley is named after Mother Mary - Maryam-Dere. Adherents of the Christian religion know the gorge because of the old Assumption Monastery that was founded in the 8th century. According to legend, it has been built by monks, who fled from Byzantium. The picturesque gorge reminded them of the home country, so they decided to start their abode there. According to another version, the monastery was built on the spot where shepherds have found the icon of Holy Mother. The latter is widely known as the Bakhchysarai icon.

Close to the place where the icon was found, the first cave temple was set. The monastery was founded later. Since its founding, the Assumption Monastery has been a special place. Even during the Russian-Turkish war it managed to avoid looting and destruction. Only in the post-revolutionary period, the monastery fell into disrepair. For several years, the neuropsychiatric boarding was situated there.

Amazing tours along the gorge are conducted for pilgrims and tourists. The length of the landmark is about 2 km. Besides the monastery, guests of these picturesque places will be able to see the wonderful mountain scenery, look at the once inhabited caves and see the remains of the rock art. Currently, the Assumption Monastery goes through another large-scale reconstruction. The renovated building looks incredibly impressive. There are lots of visitors in the monastery. All travelers can experience its unique relics and special historic atmosphere.

Odessa catacombs

Odessa catacombs are one of the biggest in the world. Its length is approximately 2,5 thousand kilometers. The main part of the underground ways are the old quarries, where stones for city building were taken. In the 19th century the catacombs have begun to build but after the revolution the rock work have to be stopped. The reason covered in a serious geological threatens.

These huge undergrounds have an outstanding history. After the revolution in 1917 they were full of criminals. Many of them weren't shut in a prison for decades because they hid deep in the underground. During the Second World War, these catacombs were the natural shielding for soviet soldiers. The most interesting labyrinths are located under the historical district of Odessa.

According to some reports, right here in the beginning of the 19th century was made the first quarry. The walls have saved the interesting epigraphs that were made by workers. Another peculiarity of catacombs is that they are united with other natural solutional caves in one complex. Natural solutional caves are interesting not only for speleologists but also for tourists. Odessa catacombs are one of the most twisted and dangerous undergrounds in the world. Even specially trained dogs can't get form them out by themselves. Today the underground tunnels are used for city needs. There are placed the warehouses of local factories and telephones.

St Andrew Church

St. Andrew Church in Kiev was built in honour of St. Andrew the First Called. It has been built for 5 years and was finished in 1754. Notwithstanding that the cathedral high is 46 meters, it looks very graceful. The building is decorated with a number of unusual Baroque style elements. There have saved grand windows and doors with a neat ornament, wonderful columns and pilasters.

The main decoration of the cathedral is the iconostasis in the Baroque style. It was made by the best masters from Saint-Petersburg. The iconostasis is made from lime. There was used gold leaf technique that made the iconostasis red that is not usual for church decoration. St. Andrew Church resembles a luxurious palace. Its halls are decorated with paintings, the walls have a lot of fretworks, also saved hundreds of years old carving.

The cathedral has placed in a quite complex geological area. Because of that there were made a lot of rebuilding works. Movement of ground waters is the reason of splits in walls. Landslides can also make a number of damages for the church. The cathedral was a victim of thunderbolts, cupolas were partly destroyed by it. The last large renewal was in 1978-1979. Several years ago, the religious monument was closed for renovation.

Leisure and attractions

Attractions and nightlife
Active vacation in Ukraine - things to do, entertainment and nightlife
The nightlife of Ukraine, especially its large cities, is colorful and multifaceted. Foreign guests can choose from a quiet atmospheric bar,

a loud groovy disco or a tech club, where non-stop events are held all night for the most energetic ones. The night club "Skybar" in Kiev is one of the most popular places where music is played all night. Stylish interior, amiable staff, delicious cocktails and complete security is what is needed to relax for those who wake up in the evening. The "Aura Beach Club" in Odessa can brag of a swimming pool, excellent music, great space, and restaurants with excellent cuisine and a large selection of dishes.

Ukraine is perfect for the fact that there is something to do here for lovers of outdoor activities all year round. Tourists who are tired of lying under palm trees on hot islands can visit Ukraine in winter and go skiing and snowboarding. During summer on the other hand, it is almost as good as the countries of eternal summer in terms of the vast choice of activities. Those who want to get closer to the Chernobyl disaster are invited to take excursions to the exclusion zone "Chernobyl Tour" and "ChernobylStore". The company "Another.Kiev" can help you to see Kiev from an unexpected side; it will take tourists to creepy abandoned buildings, booming underground ways and other similar places from which they can get goose bumps.

You can have a great time on water in the Cossack village of Migiya. It is popular among lovers of water tourism and especially rafting there are wonderful rapids, magnificent nature here, and you can also visit the Skarzhinsky water mill. Adrenaline and fresh air will be presented to you by rafting down the Stryi River, every guest of the Lviv region should try it out. Canoes or kayaks are available for vacationers who choose to visit Kiev or Zaporozhye. What could be more peaceful than to swim along the Dnieper, swim in water lilies and enjoy the beauty of the trees reflected in the water? You can rent a boat or relax on a snow-white yacht in Odessa and Mykolaiv.

Summer guests of the country who are looking for a good golf course would not have to go far. In the capital of Ukraine, there is the popular "Golf Center" overlooking the river, with a convenient well-groomed course and a good restaurant. In winter, ski resorts in Polyanytsya, Slavsky, Pilipitsa, Yasyn, Podobovets, Boryslav, Migovo and Plavie await guests there is plenty to choose from. Charming views of the snow-covered slopes of these places annually make the hearts of skiers and snowboarders beat faster. Resorts offer rental of equipment, instructions and lessons for beginners, and comfortable holiday areas.

Rope parks with zipline are gaining popularity year after year, because both adults and children sometimes want to give themselves freedom and climb for their pleasure, or fly for a spin over the boring land. There are at least four such parks in Kiev, from which visitors of all ages will leave happy and flushed. There is a "HIPPark" in Berdyansk designed in a nautical style: sails and unstable rope ladders create the impression of being on a ship during pitching. And from above opens up a view of the beach and the sea. "Bike Zip" in Bukovel is something special and even more extreme. Here the visitors literally ride the ropes on bicycles, and this pleasure is available both in summer and in winter.

Where better to fly in a balloon, if not in Kiev? Romantics will like the idea of slowly rising up into the air over the Ukrainian capital and admiring it, sailing over high buildings, trees, roads, people, and so on. Those who prefer more extreme types of leisure should go to Dnipropetrovsk, where the club "KAVA" offers customers the opportunity to jump off a bridge, play strikeball and paintball, go finally to Pripyat, and then return for a new portion of adrenaline. In "Adventure Tours" in Kiev, guests will be able to ride on a real tank, will let them shoot from automats, and also will let them enter the Exclusion Zone, which is ultra-popular and makes really high demand.

Visitors can communicate with animals in the "Uncle Bo's Ranch" in the village Nerubaysk. Here visitors will immediately notice that horses are being looked after with love. Friendly horses and ponies, which can be fed, are happy to ride adults and children under the supervision of instructors. There is also a small café here. The "Grand Prix Stud Farm" is located in Oleshka with a small cozy park, a lake, cafe and an area for children. Large celebrations are often held here, as this charming place is ideal for it. You can ride horses, take a walk in the park, and relax in a cafe while the children play in a safe playground. The place is calm and works well for people who are tired of the city.

Soul of Ukraine

Cuisine and restaurants

National cuisine of Ukraine for gourmets. Authentic recipes, delicacies and specialties

Ukraine is a country of steppes, the fertile soil of which endows Ukrainians with grain crops, as well as potato, cabbage, beetroot and other vegetables. Traditional Ukrainian cuisine includes bread products, a wide variety of vegetables and meat, mainly beef, pork and chicken. Some dishes are cooked in many different variations, for example, Ukrainians' favorite borscht can be cooked with any meat or can be cooked vegetarian style. A sour cream is often added to the borscht. The same applies for soups in general due to the huge choice of vegetables, residents of Ukraine know a large number of ways to cook soups to suit any taste.

Neighboring Poland, the homeland of sausages that Ukrainians love so much, had some influence on the Ukrainian cuisine. Meat on Ukrainian soil is generally held in high esteem: the popular cabbage rolls are stuffed with beef and rice, meat aspic is meat jelly, the piquancy of which is spiced up by herbs. Salo is used as a separate dish or in sandwich. Often Ukrainians eat okroshka, a popular Slavic dish, which is very easy to prepare. It is a cold soup prepared with chopped sausage or ham and vegetables, and then the ingredients are flooded with kvass or kefir. Sour cream and boiled eggs are added too. Such a dish is refreshing on hot days, and it has many methods of preparation. Chicken pilaf is widespread. This is a hot dish from rice, chicken and carrots, which is eaten for dinner or as a second dish during lunch.

Appetizing and fragrant potato pancakes are called "derun" or "dranik". They are popular not only because of their excellent taste, but also because of being filling, ease of preparation and availability, for the reason that only potatoes, onions, flour, eggs and vegetable oil are needed for their preparation. This dish also has variations: you can add cottage cheese, meat, mushrooms and other products. Ukrainians like potatoes fried, boiled, chopped, whole, and it is peeled before cooking or boiled with the peel. Cabbage is not inferior to potatoes in terms of popularity: it is boiled, braised, picked, and added to soups and second dishes. Ukrainians love taking a snack break with potato or cabbage pies, which are also eaten over a cup of tea.

Hombovci is buns in the form of balls, which are made of dough, cottage cheese or potatoes, often breaded. Hombovci is tasty on its own, but is even more delicious with a filling. Cherries, plums, any jam, chocolate or halva are often used as a filling. Berries, sliced fruits, jam and sweet cottage cheese wrapped in dessert pancakes are called "nalistniki". The Ukrainian version of the famous strudel, sweet roll cake, is prepared with apples, nuts and poppy seeds. Dessert dumplings with cherries are popular too. A wonderful refined cake called "flodni" was borrowed by Ukraine from Hungary. It has several fillings at once: apple, poppy and walnut.

"Uzvar" or "vzvar" is a traditional Ukrainian drink. As a matter of fact, it is water to which dried fruits, berries or herbs are added and then boiled. In ancient times, this beverage was a Christmas drink, but nowadays it is drunk at any time, especially during the hot summer. In addition to "uzvar", Ukrainians drink rye kvass during the hot season. This drink can be found in any store. Compote is a common drink, which is especially good when drinking it hot in winter. Thick ryazhenka fermented milk product, is helpful for digestion. With regards to alcohol, Ukrainians prefer the honey drink called "Medovukha", vodka with pepper and ginger called "varenukha", "spotikach" made of cherry or plum. Let us not forget the most popular and favorite drink of Ukrainians "horilka", prepared on the basis of potatoes or beets.

On holidays, Ukrainians eat fried fish, poppy cake, mushrooms, potato pancakes. It is hard to imagine a Ukrainian New Year table without the salad "Olivier", different types of sausages, and sweet donuts called "pampushki". There is also a special dish for commemoration of the deceased. It is a sweet wheat porridge called "kutya" with honey or sometimes with raisins. Table etiquette of Ukraine does not differ too much from the standard European one. Keeping your hands under the table, resting them on the seat or putting them on your knees is considered to be rude. During a feast, wrists should always be visible, but the elbows are not put on the table. As a sign of politeness, guests should ensure they eat the entire portion of the dish placed in their plate. Ukrainians often eat soup with a piece of bread. At breakfast adults eat sandwich with coffee, while children are fed more thoroughly, usually with semolina or oatmeal porridge.

It is not an acceptable practice among Ukrainians to go to cafes and restaurants often. Many working-class people and students can go to the cafe often due to lack of time for cooking, as well as to meet with friends. Ukrainians of medium and low income visit restaurants only during weddings, anniversaries and funerals, as they can rarely afford lunch or dinner in a good restaurant. Guests of the country should visit the Kievan restaurant "Hutorets na Dnipri", which serves authentic Ukrainian dishes. There is a popular restaurant in Odessa called "Dacha". In another Odessian restaurant called "Molodost", you can eat relatively cheap, but good food.

Traditions and lifestyle

National traditions of Ukraine. Habits, mentality and the way of living

Ukrainians are Slavs; more than a half of the population is Ukrainians, then Russians, Poles, Belarusians, and Romanians. Residents of

Western Ukraine speak mainly Ukrainian, while those in Eastern Ukraine speak Russian. The state language of Ukraine remains the Ukrainian language. Ukrainians are hospitable people; they like to invite guests to their home and always lay rich tables for them. The guest of a Ukrainian home brings a pie or a cake, a bouquet of flowers for the hostess and a souvenir for the kids; it is better to bring everything at once. The number of flowers in the bouquet should be strictly odd, as an even number is only suitable for the cemetery. The residents of Ukraine love long conversations; they tell stories about themselves and other people quite well. They also like to listen to someone's stories as well. Ukrainians can embarrass a foreign guest with numerous questions asked out of sheer curiosity. Ukrainians love to sing, especially during a feast.

There is no need to present expensive gifts to Ukrainian friends. Ukrainians believe that it is better to get an inexpensive, but useful gift or just something nice that displays the intention of the giver. Having received an expensive gift, a Ukrainian will consider himself in debt of the giver, or can even suspect that the guest has some mercenary motives and is trying to bribe him. Ukrainians are generous and usually in a good mood. They are temperamental, often unpredictable and poorly suppress both good and negative emotions, rely more on feelings than on reason. Most of the inhabitants of Ukraine differ in diligence and high efficiency.

The fig sign, that is, the thumb pushed through the index and middle fingers of the hand folded into a fist, is a rather rude gesture, though it is inferior in terms of level of rudeness to an elongated middle finger. It is considered indecent to point a finger at people or objects, for this they rather use all five fingers. Ukrainians are superstitious, which is why they avoid taking out the garbage in the evening, shaking hands and communicating at the doorstep, leaving empty bottles on the table. All these, according to beliefs, can lead to bad luck and misfortunes. It is forbidden to whistle indoors, especially in a residential area, in order not to be left without money. Spilled salt can lead to a quarrel, as well as the presentation of knives, scissors, and other sharp objects as gifts.

Ukrainians always take off their shoes before entering the house. They go around the house in slippers, and almost always, the hosts have at least one pair of spare slippers for guests. It is not acceptable to drink water from the tap, no matter how clean it is. Ukrainians love holidays and parties, and any occasion can become a reason for noisy celebrations. Friends and family are considered very important; they value close ties. At the same time, Ukrainians can be said to be individualists, for those who regard personal space to be important, and not just physical. This means that at least one meter of space should be maintained between unfamiliar people. If a Ukrainian decides not to open up to someone, then noting van be gotten out of him. However, he can open up everything, even the most intimate ones, to the people closest to him.

While meeting with unfamiliar and little-known persons, men shake hands, sometimes even buddies and friends greet this way. Shaking hands in gloves is not common. More often, during the greeting, close friends pat each other on the shoulders and back. Women who have not known long can shake hands. Men and women in official situations exchange handshakes too. Women welcome close acquaintances of both sexes with a kiss on the cheek. In public transport, Ukrainians are expected to give way to women with little children or heavy bags, pregnant women, elderly people of both sexes and people with disabilities. Ukrainians usually surround elderly people with honor, as it has been established from time immemorial.

The condition of Ukrainian women is two sided: on one hand, education and work are accessible to all women. They are independent, and many women work in the field of science, politics and business. On the other hand, a woman is still considered as an object. Women's views are looked down on, and jokes about women's logic and emotional instability are common. The task of cooking, cleaning the house, and taking care of the kids, is still expected from working women. Ukrainian women have a strong character, whose roots can be traced to the distant past, when the Cossacks' wives remained in charge while the husbands were engaged in military affairs.

Ukraine is known for its interesting alcohol culture. Alcoholic beverages such as horilka and medovukha seem inseparable from the image of the country. It is considered indecent to refuse to drink, and the refusal to drink at a funeral of a martyr is regarded as disrespect and even an insult to the memory of the late. Poured alcohol is expected to be drunk completely. Strong and not so strong drinks accompany all celebrations, including church holidays. Ukrainians can get drunk, but there are few drunkards among them. Basically, alcohol is considered as a means to relax in the company of friends or relatives, and people who drink alone and without reason are given the stink eye.

Family trip with kids

Family holidays with children in Ukraine attractions and entertainment

Taking children with you on a trip would be a good idea, because Ukraine can offer young travelers and their parents a lot of entertainment and equally educational programs. In Kiev, in the "Skymall" shopping center, is located "Igroland", which will entertain both children and teenagers for a whole day. For kids, there is a zone with slides, scooters and a pool with balls. You can leave your child here and sit in a cafe located right there, from where you will see your child perfectly. Older children will enjoy the carousel with horses, camels and other animals, trampolines, bowling, the maze, video games and much more. Visitors of Odessa can find something similar to "Igroland" in the shopping and entertainment complex "City-Center". Here you will find constructors, a rock for climbing, a sandbox, a rope town and other safe entertainments.

In Mykolaiv, there is a wonderful amusement park "Skazka" ("the fairytale"). A real fairy tale awaits the little guests on every square centimeter: here you can swim, ride, climb, swing, and delve in the sand. In the evening, the darkening park is enlivened with truly fabulous lighting. You can simply take a walk here, eating cotton candy and admiring the wonders that are in this park at every step. There are paid as well as free amusement rides in "Skazka". The cleanliness of the territory is closely monitored, likewise the safety of visitors. The theme park "Kievan Rus" in Kopachev is a place for entertainment and education, where there are exact copies of ancient Russian buildings. Festivals with equestrian theater, battles, dances and other performances, are also held here. You can ride horses, participate in archery, fly by zipline, go in the historical museum, take a break and have a snack in the café, all in the park. The park is open on weekends and public holidays.

Those who like playing in water can go with the whole family to the Kiev aqua park "Dream Island", located in the shopping center "Dream

Town". The aqua park is decorated in the theme of "Jurassic period", which means that it would be especially joyful for both young and adult lovers of dinosaurs. Open daily from 11am to 10pm, the aqua park offers many slides, five pools, among which is a pool with artificial waves, as well as a Jacuzzi, lots of attractions, a lagoon, rest areas, and of course, dinosaurs here and there. Akvapark "Terminal" in Brovary is not large, but it has everything necessary so as to have a good time: artificial waves, excellent slides, pleasant water and a bar. There is a huge aqua park in Kirillovka called "Treasure Island", with a large number of attractions, a pirate ship, a cafe, a restaurant and a pizzeria, a first-aid post and a souvenir shop.

Kiev has a museum which should not be missed by guests of the capital who came to have a pleasant getaway with children. This is an interactive "Experimentarium", full of illusions and puzzles, mechanisms and mirrors, magnets and lasers, musical instruments and much more. Here children learn amazing facts about the human body and the laws of physics. They will also get acquainted with chemical reactions and the work of machines, be able to express themselves, and communicate with other children science, communication, creativity and entertainment go side by side, and this is the best way to learn. Another wonderful museum in Kiev is the Museum of Water, in which group excursions are held for children in different languages. In some parts, the museum is interactive; there is an aquarium with big fish, exhibits that demonstrate the water purification system. The mission of the museum is to teach children to appreciate water and not waste it.

A visit to such an informative place as the Museum of Nature in Kharkiv cannot be missed. Here guided tours are conducted for groups, during which visitors will see many exhibits, including stuffed animals and skeletons of extinct animals what a wonder it would be to see a mammoth's skeleton. There is the National Museum of Natural History in Kiev. Five of its floors are filled with animals, birds, insects, and inhabitants of the deep sea. There is also a paleontological hall.

Communication with animals is always beneficial to both children and adults. Therefore, an excellent key would be to visit the "Feldman EcoPark" in Lesnoy. This is a wonderful place where it is good to walk in winter, and in summer, the park is transformed among the lush greenery. There are bike trails laid in the park, a variety of activities are organized on its territory, and guided tours are held too. The main thing here however, is that under the care of professionals who love nature, live turtles, snakes, eagle owls, parrots, lamas, deer, jaguars, bears, chimpanzees, hamadryas baboons and other animals. Active and fearless teens would probably like to try themselves in a rather young kind of sport wakeboarding. You can learn to perform tricks on the water with the help of a wakeboard. Jumping like a dolphin is much more fun and cool than any other water sport. It is easy to find places in Kiev, where wakeboarding is taught, and the Park of Peoples Friendship is one of such places.

Shopping

Shopping in Ukraine outlets, shopping streets and boutiques
Fancy shopping centers with expensive brands' shops, noisy markets where sounds mix, colors and smells, cozy departmental stores hidden in yards and basements, selling vintage treasures for nothing Ukraine can offer all of these and even more. The popular shopping center "Gulliver" in Kiev is one of the biggest in the country. It is full of shops of famous brands, both expensive and average in terms of prices. There is also a large supermarket in the basement. You can find in the mall too, a fitness center, bowling, children's area, bar, cinema, many cafes and restaurants. In Kherson there is a shopping center called "Fabrika". Despite its not very interesting name, this building has roots in the Soviet past, and the mall will not let you get bored. Here is a large selection of clothes and shoes of popular brands, a supermarket, children's area with trampolines, and cinemas.

The legendary market "Privoz" in Odessa has a nearly two-century history. Fresh vegetables and fruits, flowers, fish, shrimps, cheese, meat, sweets, spices, honey, clothes the huge selection of goods can confuse an inexperienced guest of the bustling Odessian market. You can also see wonderful colorful characters of Odessian people, both as buyers and as traders. Merely taking a walk through this place is already a small adventure in itself and a guaranteed mood boost. It is only important not to forget to keep an eye on your pockets. The market is mostly covered. It is open from Tuesday to Sunday, from 8am to 5pm.

The famous "Courage Bazar" in Kiev is a monthly flea market where you can find the most incredible and unexpected things. Every time a buyer thinks that nothing can surprise him, the market shocks him again. Hundreds of traders come here to sell used and new clothes, jewelry, tableware, table lamps, and watches this is the place where you can really watch the fusion of vintage and ultramodern, ordinary and strange, taking place. Let us not forget to mention, the food here is always varied and wonderful. There are musicians performing on the market, and there are areas for having a rest. In a word, people go there not only for shopping, but also for rest, socializing, entertainment and impressions. There is "Manufactura" in Khodosovka village, which is not far from Kiev. It is not even a market, but an outlet-town filled with Dutch style two-storey houses where you feel pleasure walking along the well-groomed neat streets of the city. Quality products are sold at low prices in the shops, and there is a cafe or a restaurant in every house.

Everybody likes the "Bookin" shop in Odessa, both locals and foreigners who love to read and just collectors of books. Here you can find unique books, both old and new. The assortment is very large and varied; an embarrassment of riches. You can come across rare books here. Lovers of comics should have a look into the Odessa's "On the Bus". From the "Marvel" comics and less known editions from the middle of the last century, to manga and comics of Russian authors the choice is really great, and the atmosphere of the store will not allow you to leave it earlier than after an hour. Even those who do not plan on buying anything and do not like "visual novels" will not leave the store empty-handed.

The "Pravda B" gallery in Lviv is an unusual art museum-shop filled with unique pieces of modern art. This simply means that not everyone will like it. But still, many, rejecting prejudices, will be able to find here something they like: jewelries, clothes, fabrics, books. There is another Lvivian shop which tourists cannot help but fall in love with at first sight. We are referring to "Koza Dereza". The atmosphere in this shop-workshop that sells things with clear ethnic motives is charming and calming. Here you can find Easter wreaths, Christmas tree decorations, tea sets for gift, and real embroideries. The characters in here are easily recognizable: The Nutcracker, Gerda, Little Red Riding Hood and other heroes from folk and authorial fairy tales loved since childhood.

There is a shop "Mriyi Mariyi" in Kiev, which will be a good idea to buy memorable ethnic souvenirs from: ceramics, clothes, jewelries, paintings, dolls, decors and many other things. All products are of a high quality, and the interior of the store itself looks like a lovely souvenir. At the souvenir shop of the capital "Folkmart", customers will find books, paintings, dishes, toys, magnets simply put, a lot of interesting things that capture the history and culture of Ukraine. There are also two more shops in Kiev that cannot be missed. The first one is the cozy "Dobro Store" which sells Ukrainian hand-made goods: toys, socks, and jewelries. You can also buy natural honey and sweets here. The second is the vinyl store "Diskultura", in which, it seems that there are records of all possible genres and of all possible eras. It is a find for both fashionistas and retrogrades.

For a souvenir to become a really pleasant reminder of your trip, it is necessary that it be real and has the character of the country in which it was purchased. A good souvenir from Ukraine can be an embroidered blouse. Traditional Ukrainian dresses are very beautiful. The ceramic products in each region of the country have their own characteristics; you just need to choose what you like more. Handmade products made of wool will be a beautiful and practical souvenir; these are mainly socks and blankets. Ukrainian Easter painted-eggs do not look like others. A "motanka" doll with a sun instead of a face is a "protector" that has centuries old history. From among treats you can take Carpathian tea and Lviv chocolate from Ukraine.

Tips for tourists

Travel tips for Ukraine what to prepare in advance and what to obey

1. If you want to give flowers to a Ukrainian woman, you need to make sure that it is an odd number of flowers. An even number of flowers in a bouquet is suitable only for funerals, and such carelessness can offend a Ukrainian woman. If she is superstitious, it could even frighten her. Do not present expensive gifts to a Ukrainian, even if it is from the heart. The Ukrainian, having received a gift, which by his standards is too expensive, will consider himself obliged to the presenter. He may also be suspicious and decide that the one who presented such a gift is devising something and wants to bribe him (the receiver) in advance. Also, do not buy things for unborn children, even if they seem necessary. Many Ukrainians see it as a bad omen. You cannot give knives and other sharp objects as a present, as this is a sign that the giver and the receiver will quarrel soon. Handkerchiefs are not presented either, because it is believed that the handkerchief received as a gift will bring tears. There is no need to give mirrors either. If you decide to present a wallet to a Ukrainian, you first need to put some money in it; the smallest coin will do — to attract money.

2. It is point-blank unheard of to confuse and mix Ukrainians and Russians, Ukraine and Russia, for obvious reasons this is simply insulting. The height of disrespect will be to call these countries the same or declare that Ukraine is part of Russia.

3. If you want to whistle in the room, you need to make sure that no one is nearby. Whistling in the house, even virtuously, prophesies financial problems for its occupants and the whistler himself. Some Ukrainians treat whistling in non-residential premises with prejudice as well.

4. Entering the house or apartment of a Ukrainian, you should immediately take off your shoes. The vast majority of Ukrainians have spare slippers for guests. Wiping the soles on the doormat is unacceptable, street shoes will not be tolerated here they won't let you seat at the table for sure.

5. Upon meeting you should shake hands firmly, maintaining eye contact, especially when it comes to business partners. A strong handshake symbolizes confidence, and an open look honesty. A person with wandering eyes or dull eyes does not command trust.

6. Women go to Orthodox churches with covered heads and in skirts, which must cover their knees. Men on the other hand take off their hats in the church. Shorts, open shoes and bright T-shirts are not allowed, no matter how hot it is. In churches and temples, it is forbidden to take pictures, talk on the phone, or even talk in general.

7. Never congratulate a person on his birthday before the date, or even celebrate the event in advance. This is considered a bad sign, not promising the celebrant anything good. Some people even believe

that this may reduce a person's life. To congratulate a person and celebrate the birthday in areas does not presage anything bad.

8. The fig sign is considered a rude gesture; you should not point a finger at a person or an object. If you want to make an indication, you can use all fingers of the open palm. It is acceptable to beckon on somebody with one finger-gesture only if this somebody is an animal. In cafes and restaurants you should not click your fingers when calling for a waiter this is very rude.

9. Those who refuse to drink in the company of others may be looked at askantly and the refusal written off as snobbery. Some hosts will be gravely offended if guests refuse to drink with them. Usually they drink to the health of those who are present at the gathering, if other toasts are not offered. If you had a chance to attend such a sad event as a commemoration, you cannot refuse a shot of vodka. Everyone must remember the departed; refusal will be considered as an insult to his memory. For those who for some reason completely reject alcohol, it is better to mention it immediately to the new Ukrainian acquaintances as soon as the topic to join in a feast approaches.

10. You should not refuse eating on a visit, and you must certainly eat the entire portion served you. If the guest does not eat any product, he needs to inform his host of it politely immediately upon receiving the invitation.

11. Ukrainians know that some not very educated residents of the USA and some European countries are barely familiar with the fact of the existence of Ukraine. It would therefore be a good idea to get acquainted with the culture of the country before your trip and learn a few phrases in the language. The Ukrainians will be flattered.

12. Neither the city streets, nor nature can be littered. While walking among the beauties of Ukraine, you should not pick flowers or stomp plants. This is also a manifestation of respect towards a hospitable country.

13. You should know in advance the phone numbers of taxi services or install their applications. Taxi drivers waiting for customers at spots where many tourists are, can deceive unsuspecting foreigners by inflating the price and this is not the worst possible consequences.

14. Buying food near the subway is not the best thing to do; it often turns out to be of poor quality and may simply be dangerous.

15. In public places you should not bring out money, telephones, or cameras. In general, it is worth keeping an eye on your pockets and bags.

The End

Printed in Great Britain
by Amazon

45097000R00184